Tell Me MORE

Devotional

365

Devotions for Young Girls

B&H KIDS

Nashville, Tennessee

1

The Bible Is True

God—his way is perfect; the word of the LORD is pure. *2 Samuel 22:31*

I like stories about make-believe things. Make-believe stories are about make-believe people. I also like stories about true things. True stories are about real people and really happened.

Anything you read in the Bible is real. The Bible is all true. Every part of the Bible is true. The Bible is God's message to you. God is perfect. He does not lie. His message is perfect too. You can believe the Bible.

Dear God,
Help me to believe
all of the Bible.

Jesus and the Old Testament

Everything written about me [Jesus] in the Law of Moses, the Prophets, and the Psalms must be fulfilled. *Luke 24:44*

Jesus was with His disciples for 3 years. They heard Him teach and saw Him heal. He taught them how to pray and to love others.

When Jesus came back to life, He met with them to teach them more. Jesus showed His followers that all of the Scriptures point to Him. Jesus fulfills all of God's promises!

**Dear Jesus,
Thank You for the Bible
that points me to You.**

3

You Have Proof

After he [Jesus] had suffered, he also presented himself alive to them by many convincing proofs. *Acts 1:3*

Have you ever wished you had proof that Jesus is alive? The good news is that you do have proof. A lot of people saw Jesus after He came back to life. Reports of those appearances are in the Bible. Although you did not see Him with your own eyes, you can know that what the Bible says about Jesus is true.

One reason God gave people the Bible is so they could know that Jesus is really alive.

Dear God,
Thank You for proof
that Jesus is alive.

The Word

*When you received the word of God . . .
you welcomed it . . . as it truly is, the
word of God. 1 Thessalonians 2:13*

Rodney listened to the preacher. The preacher read Bible verses that said every person chooses sin sometime in his life. He read that sin brings death, but God gives eternal life. Rodney knew he had sinned. He wanted to stop sinning.

The preacher read how Jesus died to pay the penalty for sin. Rodney prayed that God would forgive his sin and be the Lord of his life. Rodney knows the Bible is God's message to us all.

Dear God,
Help me welcome
Your message
in the Bible.

5

He Didn't Wait

While we were still helpless, at the right time, Christ died for the ungodly. *Romans 5:6*

Did Jesus wait until people were doing right before He died for them? Did Jesus wait until people stopped sinning before He died for them?

No! Jesus knows people are helpless to save themselves from the punishment of sin. He knows they are helpless to stop sinning on their own. So Jesus waited for the right time to die for sinners even though they were still sinning. Jesus died to pay the penalty for your sin.

Dear Jesus,
Thank You for
dying for sinners.

Victory!

Thanks be to God, who gives us the victory through our Lord Jesus Christ! *1 Corinthians 15:57*

When you hear the word *victory*, what do you think? Do you think about winning a race or a game? Do you think about wearing a medal or a ribbon?

Christians have a different kind of victory through Jesus. They have victory over sin because God paid the penalty for them. They have victory over death because believers in Jesus will go to heaven when they die. Jesus' birth, life, death, and resurrection made it possible for you to have that victory.

Because God sent Jesus, we have victory!

Dear God,
Thank You for
sending Jesus
as the Savior.

Ezra Helps

They sang with praise and thanksgiving to the LORD: "For he is good; his faithful love to Israel endures forever." *Ezra 3:11*

For many years, the people of Judah turned away from God. They did not obey God. So God allowed them to be taken away from their home. After 70 years away from their home, God used a special priest named Ezra. Ezra's name means "help." Ezra helped them obey and turn back to God. Ezra taught them what God wanted them to do. Ezra helped the people of Judah obey God again.

**Dear God,
Help me obey You.**

8

Lessons Learned

He went up on the mountain, and after he sat down, his disciples came to him. Then he began to teach them. *Matthew 5:1–2*

"Mom, I love my new Bible class teacher. He always smiles. He loves to teach," said Joel.

"If you enjoy what you are doing, others will notice," replied Mom.

Jesus' disciples learned from Him. The disciples knew Jesus loved His Father. Jesus enjoyed teaching about God. Some lessons made them think differently. The disciples listened to Jesus because He taught them about God.

Dear God,
I want to learn
lessons from You.

Ezra Studies

Now Ezra had determined in his heart to study the law of the LORD, obey it, and teach its statues and ordinances in Israel. *Ezra 7:10*

To learn how to do something you have to study. Ezra studied the Bible, sometimes called the "law of the Lord." He also obeyed the Bible. He taught others so they could obey too. Ezra wanted to live like God wanted him to live. Ezra wanted the people of Israel to live like God wanted them to live also.

**Dear God,
Help me study the
Bible and live like
You want me to live.**

10

Follow the Leader

If anyone serves me, he must follow me. Where I am, there my servant also will be. If anyone serves me, the Father will honor him. *John 12:26*

Do you enjoy playing the game Follow the Leader? Keeping up with the leader can be fun.

Jesus teaches you about serving Him. You serve best when you follow Jesus' example. Jesus taught by being a servant. He did not mind serving when no one was looking! You act like Jesus when you serve others. Serve others and honor Jesus.

**Dear God,
Help me serve
others by following
Your example.**

11

Cupbearer Nehemiah

Then the king asked me, "What is your request?" So I prayed to the God of the heavens. *Nehemiah 2:4*

Nehemiah was a cupbearer to the king. His job was to make sure that the king's food and drink were safe. His job was great, as long as the food was good and safe. He lived in the palace and had lots of good things. Nehemiah heard that his people, the Jews, were not being treated well. He asked God what he should do. Nehemiah had faith in God.

**Dear God,
I want faith like
Nehemiah.**

12

Real Forgiveness

He went into all the vicinity of the Jordan, proclaiming a baptism of repentance for the forgiveness of sins. Luke 3:3

"Alice, were you fighting with your sister?" asked Mom.

"Yes, Mom, but it's okay. I said sorry."

"Ellie is still upset with you. Saying sorry without really meaning it is not being sorry. You need to ask for forgiveness and mean it. That's the kind of sorry that God wants," said Mom.

To follow Jesus, you have to be sorry for the bad choices you have made. God wants your life to change.

**Dear God,
When I ask You for
forgiveness, help
me truly mean it.**

Promise

Truly I tell you, anyone who believes has eternal life. John 6:47

God's promises never fail. If Jesus says people who believe in Him live forever, He means it! How do you know that you will be with Jesus in heaven? Admit you have sinned, believe Jesus is God's Son, and accept His salvation.

Dear God,
I'm glad I can be
sure about living
forever with You.

A Greater Love

God has given us eternal life, and this
life is in his Son. *1 John 5:11*

"Dad, what does it mean to love someone? I hear people talk about love," said Quentin.

"*Love* is a word used lots of different ways. When people talk about love, they are usually talking about a feeling," said Dad. "But real love doesn't change when you have a bad day. Jesus teaches that God's love is the greatest love of all. He died because He loves us."

**Dear God,
Thank You for
loving me enough
to send Jesus.**

Focused

So I sent messengers to them, saying, "I am doing important work and cannot come down. Why should the work cease while I leave it and go down to you?" Nehemiah 6:3

God told Nehemiah to rebuild the wall around Jerusalem. The job was hard. The work was slow. People tried to keep Nehemiah from doing what God asked him to do. Nehemiah did not listen to them. He listened to God and obeyed.

**Dear God,
Tell me what You
want me to do
with my life.**

Am I a Christian?

I [Jesus] am the way, the truth, and the life. No one comes to the Father except through me. John 14:6

Are you a Christian? A Christian is more than a good person. A Christian is someone who has a special friendship with Jesus. This friendship needs an invitation to get started.

When someone invites you to a party, you have to say yes before you can go. Jesus invites you to have a friendship with Him. What will you say?

**Dear God,
Help me tell others
about my friendship
with You.**

17

Under Guard

Your constant love and truth will always guard me. Psalm 40:11

Guarding the Tomb of the Unknown Soldier in Arlington National Cemetery is an important job. It's also hard! Most soldiers who apply are turned down! During their shifts, the guards take exactly 21 steps in front of the tomb. They face the tomb for 21 seconds. They reverse the position of their weapons and take 21 steps back. All day and all night!

Your Guard is better than the team at Arlington. God's love never takes a break. You can always find His truth when you pray and read the Bible.

**Dear God,
Thank You for
guarding me all
day and all night.**

How to Be Happy

The precepts of the LORD are right,
making the heart glad. *Psalm 19:8*

A *precept* is a rule. The Bible is God's Word. It is God's rule book. It is God's plan for living a good life. God made rules to teach you how to live.

God loves you. He gave you rules to keep you safe. Learn what God's rules are. Then you can live by those rules.

Dear God, Thank You for the Bible.

19

Faith and Love

In Christ Jesus . . . what matters is faith working through love. Galatians 5:6

When you ask Jesus to become your Savior, it means you put your faith in Him. Faith is your trust.

Jesus chose to die on a cross for you. He took the punishment for your sin. You spread His love to others because you are happy that God forgave your sin.

Tell others about Jesus—what He has done for you and how much He loves them.

**Dear God,
Help me tell others
about Your love.**

People in Uniform

Jesus answered them, "My teaching isn't mine but is from the one who sent me." *John 7:16*

When a man in a brown uniform parks in front of my house, I know I'm about to get a package. When I see a police car, I know I should drive carefully! The uniforms and vehicles tell me what these people represent.

Jesus explained that He came to represent God. Everything He said, did, and taught came straight from God. Everything Jesus did helped people learn about the One who sent Him.

Dear God,
I'm glad You sent
Jesus to teach
people about You.

21

Follow the Leader

They were all astounded and gave glory to God, saying, "We have never seen anything like this!" Mark 2:12

"Hey, Dad, watch Lily copy everything I do," said Cameron.

"I can see that, Cameron. A 3-year-old loves to imitate someone older. She will follow you anywhere," replied Dad.

"Dad, I just realized that I have a big job. I need to be sure I lead Lily to the right place," said Cameron.

You can be a leader for others to follow Jesus! What do your actions show about you?

Dear God, Help me lead others to You with my actions.

22

Talk to God

Don't worry about anything, but in everything, through prayer and petition with thanksgiving, present your requests to God. *Philippians 4:6*

Do you know what to do when you worry? Talk to God. God cares about you. He loves you. He does not want you to worry.

You can talk to God in the morning. You can talk to God at night. You can talk to God when you are afraid. You can talk to God when you are happy.

Dear God,
Teach me to
pray. Teach me
to trust You.

Extra Rules

Anyone who does not remain in Christ's teaching but goes beyond it does not have God. 2 John 1:9

Tired of playing Chutes and Ladders the same old way? Try some different rules. If someone rolls doubles, everyone moves five spaces. Ask for a free move if you get the next player a snack. Some people like to add to the rules. Others say that extra rules ruin the game.

There is no need to add extra rules to the commands Jesus gave. His rules are perfect!

**Dear God,
Help me follow
Jesus' rules.**

Great Blessings

If anyone wants to be first, he must be last and servant of all. Mark 9:35

Jesus taught that a great person has to serve others. You should serve all people. That's what Jesus taught in today's verse. He showed His disciples by washing their feet. Washing feet was something a servant usually did.

Jesus wants you to serve Him. When you grow up you might serve as a teacher, preacher, counselor, doctor, artist, grocer, clerk, mechanic, fireman, or another way God wants you to serve.

**Dear God,
Help me know
where You need
me to serve You.**

A Life That Pleases

Teach me your way, LORD, and I will
live by your truth. *Psalm 86:11*

All of these kids please God by serving other people.

Janice helps her little sister get dressed.

Mark helps his mom water flowers and pull weeds for an older lady in his neighborhood.

Jacob helps his dad take out the trash.

Read and study God's Word. You will discover that serving others is the life Jesus lived. Serving others is living a life that pleases God.

**Dear God,
Help me live a life
that pleases You.**

26

Follow Jesus

The one who remains in me and I in him produces much fruit, because you can do nothing without me. *John 15:5*

Jesus loves you. He wants you to love Him. Jesus wants you to learn about Him. He wants you to listen to Him. He wants you to learn how He taught people to live. He wants you to do what He says to do. He wants to help you every day. Jesus wants you to follow Him.

Listen to your parents. Listen to your pastor. Listen to your teachers. Learn about Jesus. Love Jesus. Do the things He teaches you to do.

**Dear God,
Teach me to
follow Jesus.**

Service with a Smile

I am among you as the one who serves. *Luke 22:27*

Emma enjoys helping her mom in the kitchen. Sometimes the kitchen is really messy. Emma wants to serve others. She knows serving is what Jesus wants her to do.

Jesus calls Himself a servant. Jesus was both the Son of God and a servant to people. Jesus calls us to serve Him. When you serve, you are following Jesus' example.

**Dear God,
I pray that You
will teach me to
serve You and
others every day.**

Tell Your Friends

I am not ashamed of the gospel, because it is the power of God for salvation to everyone who believes. *Romans 1:16*

Sophie and Erin were friends. Sophie did not go to church. She had never heard that Jesus loved her.

Erin knew Jesus loved her. Erin knew Jesus loved Sophie. Erin told Sophie that Jesus loved her. Sophie went to church with Erin. She wanted to learn more about Jesus. Whom can you tell about Jesus? Whom will you tell tomorrow?

**Dear God,
Help me tell my
friends about Jesus.**

Happiness Choices

God raised up his servant and sent him
first to you to bless you by turning each
of you from your evil ways. *Acts 3:26*

You will not always make the right choices. You can
ask God to show you the right choices, though.
Today's verse says that Jesus helps us make the
right choices. Jesus helps turn us away from bad
choices. How can you make the right choices?
Read your Bible every day and pray. God will show
you the best way to live.

**Dear God,
Teach me to
follow You in all
my choices.**

Just Because

Everyone who has listened to and learned
from the Father comes to me. *John 6:45*

Mikel's dad asked him to clean up his toys. Mikel's
sister was having friends over to play. Mikel said to
his dad, "It's not my friends who are coming over!"

You may be asked to do things that help other
people. We should obey God and help others. Jesus
taught that you should obey God just because you
love Him and want to please Him.

Dear God,
Help me do
what is right.

31

Thanks to Whom?

Give thanks to the LORD; call on his name; proclaim his deeds among the peoples. *1 Chronicles 16:8*

"We made a paper chain at Sunday school today by listing things we are thankful for," said Cayden. "Our chain went all the way around the room!"

"What fun!" Mom said. "Whom would you thank for those things?"

"My parents," Cayden answered. "I guess God too."

"A lot of people talk about being thankful. However, many people forget that God is the One who gives," Mom added.

Cayden said, "I won't forget. I'll remind my friends too!"

**Dear God,
Thank You for all
the things You
have given me.**

The Faith Chapter

Without faith it is impossible to please God,
since the one who draws near to him must
believe that he exists and that he rewards
those who seek him. *Hebrews 11:6*

Hebrews 11 is often called "The Faith Chapter." The writer of Hebrews lists Bible people who showed great faith in God.

Today's verse explains that you need faith to please God. *Faith* is trusting that God is who He says He is and will do what He says He will do.

Dear God,
Please help me
have faith in You.

Have Mercy

His mercy is from generation to generation on those who fear him. Luke 1:50

"Kyle, you forgot to feed the cat, but I did it for you," said Kyle's big brother, Marcus. "Please try to remember your chores."

Kyle replied, "Usually you get mad if you have to do one of my chores."

"I'm doing what my teacher taught last week," Marcus said. "He said to think about what Jesus would do and then do it. I know that Jesus forgave. He always showed mercy to people."

Kyle said, "I'm glad Jesus sets a good example for both of us!"

**Dear God,
I'm glad You show
mercy. Help me
do the same.**

Anywhere I Go

Look, I am with you and will watch over you wherever you go. I will bring you back to this land, for I will not leave you until I have done what I have promised you. *Genesis 28:15*

I want to explore the deepest parts of the ocean, Joel thought. *I could go places no one has ever been!*

Joel's best friend, Samuel, wanted to explore outer space. Joel knew Samuel wanted to go farther than anyone had gone before.

Will God be in those places? Joel wondered. Then he remembered the Bible verse he learned last week. God promised to be with him no matter where he went—deep oceans or deep space!

**Dear God,
Thank You for
being with me
everywhere!**

In the Synagogue

He came to Nazareth, where he had been brought up. As usual, he entered the synagogue on the Sabbath day and stood up to read. *Luke 4:16*

"I like church," Ellie said. "I really like the music."

Ellie's friend asked, "Do you go to church a lot?"

Ellie laughed. "We go almost every Sunday. My parents started taking me to church when I was a baby."

Aunt Stephanie joined in. "The Bible tells us that Jesus regularly went to the synagogue to worship. Going to church every week is one of the ways I can do what Jesus did. "

"We can too!" Ellie and her friend agreed.

**Dear God,
Help me make
going to church a
normal thing I do.**

36

Talking with Jesus

While they were discussing and arguing, Jesus himself came near and began to walk along with them. Luke 24:15

"Wouldn't it be great if we could walk with Jesus?" asked Randy. "We could ask Him anything!"

"You can walk and talk with Jesus," Randy's mom said. Seeing the surprised look on Randy's face, his mom continued. "Jesus talks to you through the Bible and through prayer. He is always with you and always listens to you. He is always ready to help."

"I never thought about it that way," Randy responded. "This is great!"

**Dear God,
Help me remember
that I can talk to
You at any time.**

Children Matter

Jesus said, "Leave the children alone, and don't try to keep them from coming to me." *Matthew 19:14*

Hallie and Luke stood in line with their teenage brother while Aunt Carissa parked the car. Two men cut in line ahead of them.

One of the men said to the other, "Don't worry. They're just kids."

Jesus told His disciples to let the children come to Him. The disciples thought Jesus was too important and too busy to talk with children. Instead, Jesus taught people how to show respect and love for children.

**Dear God,
I'm glad You love
kids. Help me show
love to other kids.**

Hard to Be Kind?

Be kind and compassionate to one another, forgiving one another, just as God also forgave you in Christ. *Ephesians 4:32*

"Being kind and forgiving is so hard sometimes!" said Jillian.

"You're right. Sometimes obeying God is very hard," Dad said. "If you have trouble putting your toys away or brushing your teeth, what do you do?"

Jillian responded, "I ask someone to help me."

"That's right. When you do not want to be kind or forgiving, you can ask God for help," said Dad. "He always helps people who ask for help to obey Him."

**Dear God,
I want to obey
You. Help me to be
kind and forgive.**

Always the Same

Jesus Christ is the same yesterday, today, and forever. *Hebrews 13:8*

Some things change quickly, like an ice cube melting on a hot summer day.

Some things take longer to change, like a seed growing into a flower.

Some things take a very long time to change, like coral forming in the sea.

Jesus never changes. The power Jesus has today, He had in the past. He will have the same power in the future. You can trust that Jesus' love, patience, and knowledge will never change.

**Dear Jesus,
Thank You that I
can trust You will
always be the same.**

40

The Promise

As he promised, God brought to Israel
the Savior, Jesus. *Acts 13:23*

"Mom, how can I know what this Bible verse means?" asked Matt. "It is about a promise, but I am not sure what the promise is."

Mom read the verse and said, "Let me explain it this way. In 2 Samuel 7:12, God promised David that He would put one of David's descendants on the throne forever. In Matthew 1:1, we can read that Jesus is the descendant of King David and will be king forever!"

"I think I understand!" exclaimed Matt.

**Dear God,
Thank You for
keeping every
promise You make.**

The Bible Says

They received the word with eagerness
and examined the Scriptures daily to see
if these things were so. *Acts 17:11*

"Did I just hear you tell a lie?" Jillian asked her younger sister.

"It was a little lie," Meg said. "I didn't want to go over to her house."

"So you think telling a little lie is okay. Let's find out what the Bible says," said Jillian. She read Colossians 3:9, "Do not lie to one another."

"I think I should go back outside and explain that I'm not sick. I'll tell her that another day is better for me to come over," said Meg. "Thank you for showing me what the Bible says."

**Dear God,
Help me do what
the Bible tells
me to do.**

God's Grace

My grace is sufficient for you, for power is perfected in weakness. 2 Corinthians 12:9

"You may invite five friends to go eat pizza for your birthday," said Mom, "or you may invite all of your friends to a party at our house."

"I want to go eat pizza," said Judith. "I do not want to choose only five friends. What should I do?"

"Pray about it," said Mom. "Ask God to help you. You can make a good choice with God's help."

**Dear God,
Help me make
good choices.**

Honor God

You were bought at a price. So glorify God with your body. 1 Corinthians 6:20

Jesus loves you. He died for the sins of all people. When you choose to love Jesus, you become part of God's family.

You honor God when you make good choices for your body. Some good choices are eating good food, exercising every day, and drinking lots of water. Your body is made up of the things you put inside it.

**Dear God,
Help me honor
You by making
healthy choices.**

Listen to God's Word

Ezra opened the book in full view of all the people. . . . As he opened it, all the people stood up. *Nehemiah 8:5*

Ezra was a man of God. He knew the Bible is important because it is God's Word. Ezra wanted the Israelites to know God and follow His rules. So Ezra taught God's people. They stood up when Ezra taught because they knew God's Word was important.

**Dear God,
Thank You for
teaching me
how to live.**

45

The Best Love!

Neither death nor life . . . height nor depth, nor any other created thing will be able to separate us from the love of God that is in Christ Jesus our Lord. Romans 8:38–39

As a child, at bedtime, I told my mother how much I loved her. She would say, "I love you more." I would answer, "No, I love you more." I thought my mother loved me more than anyone else loved me. There is one person who loves me even more. His name is God!

No one can love you more than God!

**Dear God,
Thank You for
loving me!**

Follow God

I will follow you wherever you go. Luke 9:57

Dylan cleaned his room like his mom asked.

Layla did not lie to her dad.

Luke obeyed his teacher.

You have to make a lot of choices every day. Do you always choose to obey God? You can be a good example by the way you act and what you do.

Do you share? Do you listen to your teacher? Do you tell the truth? Are you kind? Obey God at home, at school, and with your friends. Obey God everywhere you go!

**Dear God,
Thank You for
helping me obey You
no matter what.**

God Is Faithful

You are righteous concerning all that has happened to us, because you have acted faithfully, while we have acted wickedly. *Nehemiah 9:33*

When the Israelites heard God's Word, they felt sorry for doing wrong things. God had told them to turn away from their sins. God was faithful to them even though they disobeyed Him.

God is always faithful to His people. He loves you and wants the best for you.

**Dear God,
Thank You for
always being
faithful.**

48

God Chose You

You did not choose me, but I chose you. *John 15:16*

God chose to send Jesus to die for your sins. Jesus teaches you right from wrong. God chose to save you because He loves you.

God chose you to be a part of His family. God chose to teach you through the Bible. Will you choose to follow Him?

**Dear God,
Thank You for
sending Jesus
to die for me.**

49

God Will Answer

In all your ways know him [God], and he will make your paths straight. *Proverbs 3:6*

Nathan broke his mom's favorite lamp. He thought about blaming his little brother. He thought about the Ten Commandments. When Nathan's mom got home, he told her the truth.

Nathan made the right choice. Doing the right thing is not always easy. Obeying God is always the right choice.

**Dear God,
Help me obey You.**

Take Care of God's House

We will not neglect the house of
our God. *Nehemiah 10:39*

God's house is a special place. When you care for
the building, you honor God. Try some of these
ways to help care for God's house.

- Walk in the hallways. Don't run.
- Take extra bulletins to the front of the church.
- Pick up trash and put it in the trash can.

Dear God,
I promise to
treat Your house
with respect.

Love One Another

Let us love one another, because
love is from God. 1 John 4:7

Sophie played with her baby sister while her mom made dinner. She picked up her toys and put them back in the toy chest. Sophie even helped her mom make a cup of hot chocolate for her dad. Before bed, Sophie prayed for her family.

God wants you to love others. Start with your family. Do not just tell your family that you love them—show your love by your actions. Look for ways to show love to each member of your family.

Dear God,
Help me show my
love to my family
every day.

God Helps Us

God is our refuge and strength, a helper who is always found in times of trouble. *Psalm 46:1*

Everyone has troubles—big and small. Maybe your brother accidentally hit you. Maybe you feel sad because your best friend moved away. Maybe you did something you knew was wrong.

No matter what troubles you have, God can help you. Trust God to help you.

**Dear God,
Thank You for
helping me with
problems.**

53

Love the Lord

Love the Lord your God with all your heart, with all your soul, with all your mind, and with all your strength. Mark 12:30

Jesus said this is the most important rule. God put it first to show how important it is. God wants you to know how much you should love Him. How can you show your love to God?

- Choose to obey God every day.
- Choose to obey God in all things.
- Always focus on doing what is right.
- Live in a way to show your love for Him.
- Love others.

Dear God,
I love You. I want
my actions to show
my love for You.

Choose Life

Choose life so that you and your descendants may live. Deuteronomy 30:19

"Why do we have rules?" Adam's Sunday school teacher, Mr. Taylor, asked his class. "We have rules for listening. We have rules for walking in the hall and leaving the building. Our lives are full of rules to follow," Mr. Taylor continued.

Rules help you do what is right and safe. When you obey God's rules, you are doing what is good for you and for others. God gives rules because He wants what is best for you.

**Dear God,
Help me obey You.**

55

In God's Sight

Be careful to obey all these things I
command you . . . because you will be
doing what is good and right in the sight of
the LORD your God. *Deuteronomy 12:28*

Do you ever wonder what is the right thing to do?
How do you decide what to do? Do you talk to an
adult you trust? Do you ask a friend?

Obeying God is the only sure way to know you
are doing the right thing. There are two good ways
to know how to obey God: Learn what the Bible
says. Pray to God.

When you need to know what is right, God will
help you!

**Dear God,
Please help me do
the right thing
by obeying You.**

56

Follow Close to God!

I follow close to you. Psalm 63:8

My puppy follows me everywhere I go! She is happy to follow me. I am happy she wants to be with me.

What does it mean to follow God? You cannot see God or hear Him. So how can you follow Him? To *follow God* means to imitate God's ways. Find out how God wants you to act. Learn how God wants you to love others. Do the things God tells you to do.

You can learn God's ways by reading your Bible, praying, and listening to your parents.

**Dear God,
Help me learn
Your ways.**

Do What Is Right!

If you do what is right, won't you be accepted?
But if you do not do what is right, sin is
crouching at the door. *Genesis 4:7*

"God wants you to do what is right," Emma's mom
said. "Let's make a list of things that are right to do."

- Obey God's rules.
- Obey my parents.
- Forgive.
- Share.
- Help others.
- Read my Bible.
- Be kind.
- Pray.
- Be truthful.
- Honor God.

**Dear God,
Help me do the
right things.**

58

God Will Show the Way

He [God] will show him the way he
should choose. *Psalm 25:12*

"I want rainbow sherbet in a cup," Jackson said.

"I want chocolate ice cream in a cone!" Oliver
exclaimed.

You make choices every day. You make choices
all day long. Some choices are fun, like choosing
ice cream! Some choices are simple. Some choices
are difficult. You choose what to do. You choose
what to say. You choose how to behave. Making
choices is important.

How do you make choices that are healthy? How
do you make choices that are good and right? Ask
God to help you make good choices. God is wise!

**Dear God,
Help me make
wise choices.**

God Is Our Comfort

He comforts us. *2 Corinthians 1:4*

Do you remember a time when you were sad or lonely? Did someone in your family comfort you with kind words? The word *comfort* means to make you feel better.

God is like that. God can comfort you with words when you read your Bible. He can comfort you when other people say kind things to you. He can calm you. Be still and listen for the peace and comfort God can give you.

Dear God,
Thank You for
the comfort You
give to me.

Make the Right Choice

Mary has made the right choice, and it will not be taken away from her. *Luke 10:42*

Jesus was an example to His followers. Jesus was loving and kind to everyone. He always obeyed God. He always made right choices.

Martha and Mary were friends with Jesus. When Jesus came to visit them, Martha was busy cooking. Mary sat with Jesus and listened to Him. What Martha did was good, but Mary's choice was better. She chose to listen to Jesus.

Dear God,
I want to listen
to You.

Peer Pressure

You must not follow a crowd in
wrongdoing. *Exodus 23:2*

"I wish I had said no to my friends," said Grayson.

Friends can be so much fun. What happens when a friend wants you to do something wrong? Do you want to do it? You do not want your friend to make fun of you. Should you do wrong just to make your friend happy? No!

Do not choose wrong things, even if a friend does. Say no. Suggest something else to do. Encourage your friends to do what is right.

**Dear God,
Help me choose
to do what You
say instead of
what others say.**

62

Listen and Obey

Blessed are those who hear the words of this prophecy and keep what is written in it. Revelation 1:3

At church, Kaylee and Nicholas learned about obeying God's rules. Later, Kaylee talked back to her mom when she asked Kaylee to set the table. When Nicholas's dad asked him to take out the trash, Nicholas obeyed without complaining.

Both Kaylee and Nicholas listened to what the Bible said about obeying God's rules. Who chose to obey? It's not enough to know what is right. You must also do what is right. Listen and obey.

**Dear God,
Help me to learn
and do what the
Bible says.**

Serve God

It is written: Worship the Lord your God, and serve him only. *Luke 4:8*

What do you think of when you hear the word *serve*? Do you think about putting food on a plate for someone? What does it mean to serve God? You cannot hand Him food. How does God want you to serve Him? God wants you to worship Him, obey Him, and show Him respect.

You can serve God through your actions and your attitude. Remember to serve God today.

**Dear God,
Help me remember
to serve You only.**

Control Anger

Don't envy a violent man or choose
any of his ways. *Proverbs 3:31*

What do you do when someone makes you angry?
Do you yell at him? Do you call him a name? Do you
say bad things about him?

Today's verse says you should act differently
when angry. Do not do or say anything because you
are angry. Choose to control your anger by

- Walking away.
- Calming down.
- Putting yourself in time-out.
- Praying and asking God to help you.

Then you can work things out peacefully.

**Dear God,
Help me control
my anger.**

Living Word

You are the Messiah, the Son of the
living God. *Matthew 16:16*

"You are so annoying!" shouted Jill to her little sister.

"Jill," began her mother, "please do not say things like that to your sister. She may be bothering you, but that is not who she is!"

Some people use wrong words to say who a person is. Some people use wrong words to say who Jesus is. No matter what some people say, you can know Jesus is the one and only Son of God.

**Dear God,
Thank You for
Your Son, Jesus.**

Hold Strong

The LORD is good, a stronghold in a day of distress. Nahum 1:7

A *stronghold is* a safe place people go for protection. When people need protection, they run to the stronghold.

God shows His love for you by being your stronghold. He is with you no matter what is happening around you. You can know God is with you because He said He would be with you.

Dear God, Thank You for being with me no matter what is happening around me.

67

One Name

He was named Jesus—the name given by the angel before he was conceived. Luke 2:21

Choosing the name for a baby can be difficult. Parents want to get their baby's name just right. They know their baby will have this name for the rest of his life.

Mary and Joseph did not have trouble naming Jesus. An angel told them what to name their child. His name is Jesus.

**Dear God,
Thank You for
sending Jesus
as a baby.**

68

Greatest Gift

For God loved the world in this way: He gave his one and only Son, so that everyone who believes in him will not perish but have eternal life. John 3:16

When you receive a gift, it becomes yours. You can do whatever you want to do with your gift. Some gifts you use to make things. Some gifts you play with. Other gifts you may forget about or even throw away.

God gave you His greatest gift, His love. You can accept His love when you trust Jesus to be your Savior.

Dear God,
Thank You for Jesus.

Wherever You Go

Seek the LORD, all you humble of the earth, who carry out what he commands. *Zephaniah 2:3*

When you travel, how does your suitcase get from the ticket gate, to an airplane, and then to a different city? Your clothes travel from one place to another because people carry your bag through the process.

God wants you to carry His commands with you and obey them wherever you are. When you learn about and follow the Bible, God can use you to do amazing things. You can help people learn about His Word, His love, and His Son.

**Dear God,
I want to help
people know You.**

70

The Gate

Jesus answered, "Truly I tell you, unless someone is born of water and the Spirit, he cannot enter the kingdom of God." John 3:5

Many years ago castles were built with only one way into the castle area. This one way was blocked by an iron gate that would only be opened to friends and guests.

God wants to welcome everyone into His family. However, there is only one way into God's family. You become God's family when you accept Jesus as God's one and only Son. Jesus loves you and wants you to be a part of His family.

Dear God,
Thank You for giving
me a way to be
with You forever.

71

Toward God

She will give birth to a son, and you are to name him Jesus, because he will save his people from their sins. Matthew 1:21

You are here right now because you were born as a baby. You can do the things you can do because you have grown bigger and stronger. When you become a Christian, you will grow as Jesus grew.

The Bible tells us that to grow like Jesus, we have to grow in wisdom, faith, and friendships. Growing like Jesus will help you know God better and do the things He wants you to do.

**Dear God,
Help me grow
like Jesus grew!**

God Is...

Lord GOD, you are God; your words
are true. *2 Samuel 7:28*

Remembering who God is can help you to trust
Him more. God is the Creator. God is your heavenly
Father. God is your friend. God can be your Savior.
He is mighty. He is the shepherd of your life. God
lives forever. He is loving. God is faithful and won-
derful. He is merciful and forgiving.

It is important for you to know who God is to you.

**Dear God,
Thank You for
being God!**

Carry Purpose

If anyone wants to follow after me, let him deny himself, take up his cross daily, and follow me. Luke 9:23

God wants every person to live for Him. To *carry your cross* means that you do what God wants you to do. He wants you to make wise choices, treat others kindly, and tell them about His love.

Dear God,
Help me to obey
Your commands
and live like You
want me to live.

You Got It

Who then is this? Even the wind and the sea obey him! *Mark 4:41*

To learn at school, you must listen to and obey your teachers. If you like swimming at a local pool, you must listen to and obey the lifeguard. To grow up happy and healthy, you must listen to and obey your parents.

When Jesus spoke, even the weather obeyed Him. To fulfill God's purpose, He rose from the dead. So whom should all of us listen to and obey? You got it—Jesus!

**Dear God,
Help me listen to
and obey Jesus.**

Play Right

*Be careful to do everything I command you;
do not add anything to it or take anything
away from it. Deuteronomy 12:32*

What happens when you play a game with someone who likes to change the rules? The game changes.

What happens in any sport if even one athlete tries to play by his or her own rules? The game stops.

Playing life by God's rules is important. He knows and wants what is best for you. Following God allows you to experience life the way He created it.

**Dear God,
I want to live
my life following
Your rules.**

The Blessed One

Blessed is the King who comes in the name of the Lord. *Luke 19:38*

When a ruler rises to power in any country, the leader rules based on what he or she thinks is important. When a ruler is selfish, the country suffers. When a ruler is kind, the country thrives.

Jesus came to earth and will come again. He came to save us from sin. He will come again for His people. We will live with Him forever.

Dear God,
Thank You for
sending Jesus to save
people from sin.

Your Best

"If you want to be perfect," Jesus said to him, "go, sell your belongings and give to the poor, and you will have treasure in heaven." Matthew 19:21

Sharing can be hard. Giving away things that you like or love can be even more difficult. God is not asking you to give away everything and have nothing. He wants to know that you will show love to others. When you show love to others, you can help them see just how much God loves them.

Dear God,
Help me give
my best to help
others know You.

Let It Out

Hosanna to the Son of David! Blessed is he
who comes in the name of the Lord! *Hosanna*
in the highest heaven! *Matthew 21:9*

We cheer for people and things every day. People
clap and scream at games. People scream in delight
while on rides at amusement parks.

The word *Hosanna* is a shout of adoration. While
you may not use the word *Hosanna* much today,
you can show your love and excitement for Jesus
in all sorts of ways. The praise is in you. Let it out!

Dear God,
Help me show my
love for You in all
sorts of ways.

79

Tell the World

When the centurion saw what happened, he began to glorify God, saying, "This man really was righteous!" *Luke 23:47*

God created the world. He created every person who ever lived on the earth. God sent His Son, Jesus, so that every person could be saved from sin who believes. Jesus lived and died. He then rose from the dead. God continues to perform miracles and help people. God is loving and just. It's our turn to tell the world that Jesus is God's Son.

**Dear God,
Help me tell
people about
Your Son, Jesus.**

80

God Will Win

Saviors will ascend Mount Zion to rule over the hill country of Esau, but the kingdom will be the LORD's. *Obadiah 1:21*

Watching what is going on in the world today can be scary. Bad things seem to happen almost everywhere. God tells us in the Bible that people who choose to obey Him will be on the winning side. Those who do not choose to obey Him will not be on the winning side. So stay on God's side and follow Him!

Dear God,
Help me live my
life as You want
me to live.

Jesus' Love

As they were eating, Jesus took bread, blessed and broke it, gave it to the disciples, and said, "Take and eat it; this is my body." Matthew 26:26

After a person becomes a Christian, he takes the Lord's Supper to remember what Jesus did for him. God wants Christians to remember. God wants you to obey Jesus and live for Him. It is possible because Jesus gave His life for you.

**Dear God,
I want to live
my life for You.**

Rise

He is not here. For he has risen, just as he said. Matthew 28:6

What do you believe? God wants us to believe what the Bible says about an event in history that changed the world. Jesus died on a cross, and three days later, He rose again. Jesus defeated death to give us life. Through faith in Him, you will live forever with God. With God, you can conquer anything life throws your way. Trust Him!

Dear God,
Thank You for
helping me through
life's scariest times.

The Adventure

I have treasured the words from his [God's] mouth more than my daily food. Job 23:12

There are lots of stories about finding hidden treasure in books and movies. Many people are willing to do just about anything to find hidden treasure.

Discovering the treasure of God's Word is easy for those who really want to find God. The Bible is God's Word. When you read your Bible, you discover the treasure inside. When you memorize Scripture, you will remember it. You will know it is a valuable treasure.

**Dear God,
I want to treasure
Your words in
my life and live
by them.**

Number One Authority

They were . . . asking one another, "Who then is this? He commands even the winds and the waves, and they obey him!" *Luke 8:25*

When an officer in the military gives an order, soldiers obey without question. Military officers have the authority to give commands. But even the highest ranking commander cannot control nature and creation. Only one person can give orders to all of creation. That one person is Jesus. Keeping Jesus as number one in your life is important.

**Dear God,
Help me keep Jesus
as the number one
authority in my life.**

85

Coming Back

Look, he is coming with the clouds, and every eye will see him. Revelation 1:7

Watching a parade can be a lot of fun, especially when a person you know is on one of the floats. You never know when that person or float will pass by you. The excitement builds as you wait for the float's arrival.

We are waiting for Jesus to come back one day. We do not know when, but He is coming. The way you stay excited about Jesus' return is to trust Him, obey His words, and tell others what you know about Him.

**Dear God,
Help me tell people
all about Jesus.**

A Closer Look

Look at my hands and my feet, that
it is I myself! *Luke 24:39*

The disciples had a hard time believing that Jesus
had risen from the grave. Even after He rose from
the grave and the disciples saw Him face-to-face,
some still thought it was impossible. Remember,
the disciples watched Jesus die.

Then Jesus told the disciples to take a closer
look. Jesus still had the marks on His hands and
feet from being nailed to the cross. Keep learning
about Jesus. Keep obeying what you are taught.
You will see that He really is the Son of God!

**Dear God,
Help me know
and trust You.**

Shout

He answered, "I tell you, if they were to keep silent, the stones would cry out." Luke 19:40

What people learn when they dig in the ground is amazing. You can learn about people who lived long ago through what is found in rocks and dirt around the rocks.

Even if no person on earth shouted the truth about Jesus, one day everything God created will sing of God's glory. The whole earth tells His story—the story of creation and history. Do not let the rocks have to do what you were created to do. Go out and shout God's praises!

**Dear God,
I want to praise You
for Your creation.**

Keep It Flowing

Then he took a cup, and after giving thanks, he gave it to them and said, "Drink from it, all of you." *Matthew 26:27*

Your blood is amazing. Through your blood, everything your body needs to survive is delivered to every cell in your body. Your heart keeps the blood flowing and other organs help keep it clean.

Faith in Jesus works like that. When you believe in Jesus, He forgives your sin. Reading and learning about Him keeps His words flowing through your mind and heart.

Dear God,
Help me to keep
learning all
about You.

Greatest Show

When they saw him, they worshiped. Matthew 28:17

Worship is more than singing songs to Jesus in church. When you worship, you love God and obey Him. *Worship* is "to be in awe of someone or something." Worship is wanting to offer praise, honor, and respect.

What is the best way to worship Jesus? The best way to worship Jesus is to believe He truly is God's Son and obey His words. There is no greater act of worship than to obey Him.

**Dear God,
I believe Jesus is
Your Son. Help me
obey Your Word.**

Quickly

Then go quickly and tell his disciples, "He has risen from the dead." *Matthew 28:7*

What kinds of things make you want to run and tell your friends and family what just happened? Maybe something funny, strange, or amazing causes you to run and tell anyone who will listen.

Jesus taught about God. He healed people and performed other miracles. He died on a cross for our sin and rose from the dead. He went back to heaven to be with God. He sent His Spirit to help, love, and guide us. Jesus is worth talking about. Go quickly and tell others!

**Dear God,
Help me tell people
about You.**

91

It's No Joke

After he had said this, he was taken up as they were watching, and a cloud took him out of their sight. Acts 1:9

Have you played a joke on anyone lately? Has anyone played one on you?

Right before Jesus ascended to heaven, He told His disciples they would be His witnesses everywhere in the world. Wow—*everywhere*! I wonder if His disciples thought He was joking!

Jesus was not joking. He wants everyone to hear the good news about His death and resurrection. Whom can you tell about Jesus?

**Dear God,
Help me tell
someone about
You today.**

Powerful News!

He is not here, but he has risen! *Luke 24:6*

Two angels told that Jesus had been raised from the dead. Sometimes cartoons show angels with harps or halos. The Bible describes angels as powerful warriors. In this passage, the angels wear dazzling clothes. They cause others to be scared and bow to the ground. The message of Jesus' resurrection is powerful! How amazing it is that God wants us to join with His warrior angels and tell others that Jesus has been resurrected!

Dear God,
I want to tell
others that Jesus
has been raised
from the dead.

Well Pleased!

And a voice from heaven said: "This is my beloved Son, with whom I am well-pleased." *Matthew 3:17*

After John the Baptist baptized Jesus, God said that He was "well-pleased" with His Son.

Do you ever wonder if God is well-pleased with you? If you are His child, then yes, He is! Sometimes you will sin and do things that make God sad. But even when you do, He still loves you!

Dear God,
Thank You for
loving me as
Your child.

God's Got a Plan

Then he opened their minds to understand the Scriptures. *Luke 24:45*

After Jesus rose from the dead, He appeared to His disciples. They thought He was a ghost. To prove He was not a ghost, Jesus showed the disciples the scars on His hands and feet. He then showed them where the Old Testament says Jesus would suffer and rise from the grave. In the Bible, God likes to tell His plans. He wants you to understand what He says in His Word.

Dear God,
Thank You for
helping me
understand more
about You.

How Did He Do That?

When he [Peter] stooped to look in, he saw only the linen cloths. *Luke 24:12*

"Abracadabra!"

Have you ever seen a magician make someone disappear? Of course it is always a trick. A person cannot disappear.

When Peter first saw only linen cloths in Jesus' tomb, he might have thought it was a trick! But it was not. Jesus rose from the dead. There is no magic trick.

**Dear God,
Thank You for
Your power!**

Love, God

As the Father has loved me, I have also loved you. Remain in my love. *John 15:9*

Think of today's verse as a note from Jesus to you. Write your name in the blank.

Dear _____ , "as the Father has loved Me, I have also loved you. Remain in My love." Love, Jesus.

The verse says if you follow Jesus and obey Him, you will remain in His love. Pray and ask God to help you follow Jesus.

**Dear God,
Thank You for
loving me.**

Interpreting Truth

Beginning with Moses and all the Prophets,
he interpreted for them the things concerning
himself in all the Scriptures. *Luke 24:27*

Griffin watched as Jeremy moved his hands. Griffin knew the movements were sign language. Jeremy was deaf. He could not hear sound. Griffin and his other friends had learned to *interpret*, or understand, Jeremy's way of communicating.

Jesus sometimes needed to tell people things they did not understand. Jesus *interpreted*, or explained, some things in the Scriptures that His followers could not understand on their own.

**Dear God,
Thank You for
making the
Scriptures
clear to me.**

Told You So!

He also said to them, "This is what is written:
The Messiah would suffer and rise from
the dead the third day." *Luke 24:46*

Have you ever heard someone say, "I told you so"?
A person usually says this when she is proud about
being right. Jesus lovingly told His friends "I told you
so!" He wanted them to know that His resurrection
was no surprise. They may have felt surprised, but
it was told about in the Old Testament. God plans
every detail of every event.

**Dear God,
Thank You for
knowing everything
that will happen.**

99

Every Part of You

"Love the Lord your God with all your heart, with all your soul, with all your strength, and with all your mind;" and "your neighbor as yourself." *Luke 10:27*

Today's verse says to love God with your heart, soul, strength, and mind. That means you love Him with every part of you.

Heart is the place inside you where happiness, sadness, fear, and love is felt. *Soul* is the part of you that can live forever with Jesus in heaven. *Strength* is the way your body works out problems of all kinds. *Mind* is the part of you that thinks and remembers.

Whatever your emotions are, whatever your personality is, whatever you do, and whatever you think—love God.

**Dear God,
Help me love
You with every
part of me.**

100

For Us

Christ died for our sins according to the Scriptures. *1 Corinthians 15:3*

"I'll do it," Nate told his brother, Ryan. Nate said that he would help their mom clean the windows.

Ryan had disobeyed their parents. He was given extra chores as punishment. Nate offered to take the punishment for his brother and do the chores. It reminded Ryan of what he had learned about Jesus in Bible class.

When Jesus died on the cross, He did it for you and me. People sin every day, but Jesus never did. Jesus took the punishment for sins of other people! He made a way for us to spend forever with God in heaven.

**Dear God,
Thank You for
dying for my sins.**

101

Trust Me!

His disciples . . . believed the Scripture and the statement Jesus had made. John 2:22

"I did not take the cookies!" Bryan told his friends.

Bryan and his friends could not find the missing cookies anywhere. They were all sad that they would not get to eat them. But Bryan's friends believed him when he said he did not take them.

Jesus' friends believed Him. They knew they could trust Him. Do you trust what God says in His Word? You can trust Him like no one else!

Dear God,
Thank You that
I can trust
Your Word.

Day Three

He was raised on the third day according to the Scriptures. 1 Corinthians 15:4

After Jesus was crucified, He was placed in a dark tomb. He stayed there for three days. The Bible says that He died and was buried, and then on the third day, He rose from the dead! Those days were probably really sad. But there was also great news! After those long hours in the tomb, the third day was cause for a celebration. That celebration has lasted for thousands of years!

Dear God,
Thank You for being
our living God.

Prove It!

He showed them his hands and his
side. So the disciples rejoiced when
they saw the Lord. *John 20:20*

Jesus showed the disciples His hands and side so
they would believe He was crucified on the cross
and rose again. It was hard to believe that such a
thing could happen. When they saw Jesus' hands
and side, they believed that He had risen from the
dead. They were surprised and amazed!

Dear God,
Help me to believe
in You, even when
I can't see You
with my eyes.

Stay Strong!

Let us not get tired of doing good. *Galatians 6:9*

Jillian was tired. She wanted to go to bed. She had promised her little sister that she would read her a Bible story before bed. Jillian decided to read the story. When she went to bed, she felt good about keeping her promise. She helped her sister learn about Jesus.

Sometimes it is hard to do the right thing. You might get tired, or sad, or even mad. But the Bible says you must stay strong. God will help you do the right thing.

**Dear God,
Give me strength
to always do the
right thing.**

105

He Will Return

This same Jesus, who has been taken from you into heaven, will come in the same way that you have seen him going into heaven. *Acts 1:11*

The disciples were probably sad when Jesus went back to heaven. But how exciting to see Him taken to heaven! Jesus was standing with them. Then they saw Him taken up into the clouds! When Jesus returns to earth one day, He will come back that same way. He will come down from the sky! How amazing that will be!

**Dear God,
Thank You that
Jesus will return
one day!**

Number One Teacher

The Holy Spirit . . . will teach you all things and remind you of everything I have told you. *John 14:26*

Teachers are important. Think of your favorite teachers. What things about them do you like? Their love for you? The way they explain things to you? The way they help you learn to be a better person? The Holy Spirit is God's Spirit. He loves you, teaches you, and reminds you what you have learned. The Holy Spirit is the most important teacher you will ever have!

**Dear God,
Thank You for
sending Your Holy
Spirit to teach
and guide me.**

A-MAZE-ing!

There is salvation in no one else, for there is no other name under heaven given to people by which we must be saved. Acts 4:12

"This corn maze is so much fun!" squealed Ella, "but I'm lost! There is only one way out, and I cannot find it."

Have you ever tried to walk through a maze? In a maze, there is usually only one way out. Much the same way, there is only one way to heaven. Jesus is that one way to heaven. When you believe in Jesus and put your trust in Him, you become a Christian. You have salvation and will be with Jesus in heaven one day.

**Dear God,
Thank You for
providing a way for
me to go to heaven.**

Hope = Strength

Be strong, and let your heart be courageous, all you who put your hope in the LORD. *Psalm 31:24*

The rope hung high in the gym. It was a long way to the top, but Emma thought she could climb it. At the top was a bell. Emma knew that she could not get to the bell on her own. She prayed that God would help her to be strong and brave. She climbed and climbed and reached for the bell. "Ding!" The bell rang loud and clear. Emma thanked God for helping her make it to the top. Emma learned that God helps people be strong and brave any time.

**Dear God,
Help me always put
my hope in You.**

Love It!

"I have loved you," says the LORD. *Malachi 1:2*

We use the word *love* every day. We say we love pets, songs, and candy. Those things are great, and we like them a lot. God's love is much more than just fun. Put a check mark by the things that you like, and draw a heart by the things that God says you should truly love.

_____Ice cream   _____Your friends

_____Clothes   _____Movies

_____Sunny days   _____God

_____Your family   _____Pizza

_____The Bible

**Dear God,
Thank You for
loving me! Help
me love others.**

110

Not the End

This has now been made evident through the appearing of our Savior Christ Jesus, who has abolished death and has brought life and immortality to light through the gospel. *2 Timothy 1:10*

The End—those words show that a book is over. When something is over, it stops. Death means the end of a life. But the end of a life does not have to mean the end forever. Jesus made a way for death not to be the end. When you trust Jesus, you become a Christian. A Christian's life will never be over. Even when a Christian's body dies, his soul will live forever in heaven with Jesus.

**Dear God,
Thank You for
providing a way
for me to live with
You forever.**

What's in a Name?

These are written so that you may believe that Jesus is the Messiah, the Son of God, and that by believing you may have life in his name. John 20:31

What is your name? Maybe your parents told you why they gave you that name. Have your parents told you what your name means? If they have not told you, ask them! A name is very special.

Jesus' name is the most special and perfect name of all. Today's verse says that if you believe in Jesus, you will have life in His name. When you become a Christian, you accept the life He gives.

**Dear God,
Thank You that
I can have life
in Your name.**

Attention, Please!

Remember Jesus Christ, risen from the dead and descended from David. *2 Timothy 2:8*

"Jackson, pay attention!" Jackson's mother said.

Jackson was trying to finish cleaning his room. He could hear his friends playing and could not wait to go outside!

Sometimes it is hard to pay attention. The Bible teaches that you should keep your attention on Jesus all the time. Many things can distract you, but focusing on Jesus is important.

**Dear God,
Help me keep my
mind on You.**

What in the World?

All the nations of the earth will be blessed
by your offspring because you have
obeyed my command. *Genesis 22:18*

Do you listen to God, your parents, and teachers? God wants you to obey Him. Abraham obeyed God, and God is blessing every nation because of Abraham's obedience. Today, almost 200 countries exist in the world. All of them will be blessed because one man obeyed God!

God wants you to obey Him. Obedience can make a difference, not just for you, but for people all over the world!

**Dear God,
Remind me to
obey You.**

Monitor the Situation

For his eyes watch over a man's ways, and he observes all his steps. Job 34:21

When you were a baby, your parents probably put a baby monitor in your room. A baby monitor allows parents to watch over their children when they are not in the same room.

God is always with you wherever you go. He can see and hear you, even without a monitor! No camera or monitor anywhere in the world can see, hear, or protect you as well as God!

**Dear God,
Thank You for
watching over me.**

Right–Hand Man

Jesus . . . endured the cross, despising
the shame, and sat down at the right hand
of the throne of God. *Hebrews 12:2*

Are you right-handed or left-handed? Many people
in the world use their right hand more than their left.

Jesus lived on earth and died on a cross. Jesus
was then given a position at the right hand of God.
Sitting on the right-hand side of a king is an honor.
God gave that important spot to Jesus.

Dear God,
Thank You for Jesus.

Choosing to Forgive

If you forgive people their offenses, your heavenly Father will forgive you as well. *Matthew 6:14*

Janna sat on the edge of her bed. She thought about what Kara said. Why would she lie? Janna felt angry one minute. She felt sad the next. But she knew to trust God and do what is right.

Janna smiled as she thought about what she would say to Kara: *Jesus forgave me for doing wrong. I choose to forgive you for lying to me.*

**Dear God,
Thank You for
forgiving me
of my sins.**

A Real Treasure

Paul . . . reasoned with them from the
Scriptures, explaining and proving that it
was necessary for the Messiah to suffer
and rise from the dead. *Acts 17:2–3*

How do you take care of something valuable? Do
you think of it often and keep it safe?

You are the most valuable treasure to Jesus. He
thinks of you. He watches over you all the time. He
even gave His life to rescue you. But there is more.
He rose from the dead so you could have a new
life with Him. He is preparing a place in heaven for
everyone who trusts Him.

When you look at a picture of yourself, remember
how much Jesus values you!

**Dear God,
Thank You that
You value me.**

Thumbs Up

As we have opportunity, let us work for the good of all. *Galatians 6:10*

Coach asked Jonathan to pitch in the game. But Jonathan knew his team had a better chance of winning if David pitched. Jonathan said a prayer. *What should I do?* he prayed. Then he knew. He spoke to Coach and tossed the ball to David.

Jonathan encouraged David, and his team won! More importantly, he and David became good friends.

**Dear God,
Help me do what
You say is best!**

119

Tell It Again

Every day in the temple, and in various homes, they continued teaching and proclaiming the good news that Jesus is the Messiah. Acts 5:42

If your team won a game, would you want to tell anyone? You would probably tell your friends and your grandparents.

Peter and the other disciples could not stop telling people the good news about Jesus. They wanted everyone to know that Jesus had died and was alive again.

Jesus offers you a new life. His good news is always worth telling.

**Dear God,
Help me tell the
good news about
Jesus every day.**

Always Listen to God

Whoever listens to me will live securely. *Proverbs 1:33*

King Solomon was a wise man because he asked God to give him wisdom. He knew that wisdom only comes from God. People visited from faraway places to ask for his advice. King Solomon told the people that they could be safe and secure by listening to God. You can do the same.

Dear God,
Thank You for Your
promise to keep
me safe and secure
when I listen to You.

121

Messiah, Our Savior

This Jesus I am proclaiming to you
is the Messiah. *Acts 17:3*

One year my best friend and her family promised to take me on a trip with them to Texas. I could hardly think of anything else. Finally, just as they promised, they picked me up. We had a wonderful vacation!

God made a much greater promise. When Adam and Eve sinned, God promised to send the Messiah to take away the sins of all people. Thousands of years passed. Then finally, Jesus came to earth as the Messiah—the Savior sent by God to save people from their sin.

Dear God,
Thank You for
sending Jesus.

In His Steps

Be imitators of God, as dearly loved children. Ephesians 5:1

My grandfather had big feet. I used to follow him out in the field. I had to take big steps to step in his footprints. I watched each step carefully. I wanted to be just like him.

God wants you to be like Him. That is why He created you in His image. How can you imitate God? God is love. You can love others like God loves them. Instead of mean words, you can say kind words. You can be caring and forgiving. Then others will see God in you.

**Dear God,
Help me love
others as You do.**

Encouraging Words

I commit you to God and to the word of his grace, which is able to build you up. Acts 20:32

"Did Mom say you could not go to Jenny's birthday party?" Ben asked.

His sister, Shelby, sat on her bed crying. She nodded. "I feel bad because I yelled back at Mom," Shelby said.

Ben remembered what the Bible says. "I know what will make you feel better," he said. "Tell God how you feel, and ask Him to forgive you. Then tell Mom."

When you tell others about God's love and forgiveness, they can be encouraged to do what is right.

**Dear God,
Thank You for
encouraging me
through the Bible.**

124

Make More Friends

Accept one another, just as Christ also accepted you. Romans 15:7

New neighbors moved in next door. Mom noticed a boy Jake's age sitting in the yard, looking sad.

"Jake," called Mom. "I will smile all day if you can make friends with our new neighbor."

Jake ran to the garage and grabbed a ball. He threw the ball in the air a few times to get the boy's attention. The boy jumped up and ran out to catch a toss. Soon they were laughing. As Jake introduced Liang to his other friends, he saw Mom smiling.

God is pleased when you show love by accepting others too.

**Dear God,
Help me show
Your love by
accepting others.**

125

I'm Back!

"Return to me, and I will return to you,"
says the LORD of Armies. *Malachi 3:7*

Have you ever been on a fun trip? After a while, did you become homesick? Did you miss your home and friends? God misses you when you do not spend time with Him. He wants you to talk to Him. He wants you to read His message to you in the Bible. God wants to spend time with you because He loves you. Did you know He wants to have a close relationship with you? He promises that He will always be close to you if you will just spend time with Him.

**Dear God,
Help me grow
closer to You.**

Busy Body!

Jesus began . . . preaching the good news of the kingdom, and healing every disease and sickness among the people. *Matthew 4:23*

The human body is amazing! In just 24 hours, your blood travels the distance from North Carolina to California four times!

God made our incredible bodies, and He cares about whether our bodies are healthy. He cares so much that He sent Jesus to die and rise again to conquer sin, sickness, and death.

Dear God,
Thank You for
providing perfect
eternal life in Your
heavenly kingdom.

Decide for Yourself

For a whole year they met with the church and taught large numbers. The disciples were first called Christians at Antioch. *Acts 11:26*

"Your sister has been talking to me about becoming a Christian," Mom said.

"Isn't she already a Christian? You and Dad are," Abbey said.

"A person is not a Christian because her parents are. Brianna trusted Jesus to forgive her of her sins. One day God will ask you to trust Jesus. Then you will decide if you want to become a follower of Jesus."

Dear God,
Thank You for
people who teach
me about Jesus.

128

Show God Love

The one who has my commands and keeps them is the one who loves me. *John 14:21*

My mother used to read the Bible to me at bedtime. Before I prayed, I would ask, "Mom, was I a good boy today?" I really wanted to hear her say yes. I loved her and hoped that I had obeyed her each day. I also wanted to obey God before I talked with Him.

If you obey God, you show Him your love. God sees your love for Him when you do what He commands.

**Dear God,
Have I obeyed
You today? Help
me love and obey
You every day.**

Stories with a Lesson

Jesus told the crowds all these things
in parables. *Matthew 13:34*

Jesus loved to tell stories or parables to teach people. A *parable* is an earthly story with a heavenly
meaning. He told parables about seeds and weeds.
He taught about hidden treasures and pearls. He
told a parable about a lost sheep. You can read over
thirty of His parables in the Bible.

Parables were meant to be more than stories to
enjoy. Jesus wants you to think about the parables
He told. Ask Him to help you understand what each
parable teaches. When you remember that Jesus
created everything, you can realize that He under-
stands everything. You can trust Him to teach you
how to live.

**Dear God,
Teach me how
to live.**

130

Show by Serving

So if I, your Lord and Teacher, have washed your feet, you also ought to wash one another's feet. John 13:14

Andrew ran upstairs yelling, "Dad! Someone is mowing our yard!"

Dad propped himself up in bed. "I know," he replied, smiling. "Do you recognize him?"

Andrew looked. "Pastor Norman?"

"Yes," said Dad. "When he came by to see how I was after the surgery, he noticed the lawn. He asked if he could cut the grass for me."

God wants you to do more than teach others about His love. Serving others is a way to show God's love.

**Dear God,
Help me show
Your love by
serving others.**

Faith, Not Fear

Jesus spoke to them. "Have courage! It is I. Don't be afraid." *Matthew 14:27*

I dreaded going to recess. I was afraid of a bully. When my older sister heard, she promised to watch out for me. After that, I stopped hiding from the bully. I told the bully I was not afraid of him and offered to share my lunch with him.

When you are scared, remember that Jesus is always with you. He can replace your fear with faith in Him. Faith in Jesus chases away all fear.

Dear God,
Give me faith in You.

Feeling Thankful

One of them, seeing that he was healed, returned and, with a loud voice, gave glory to God. Luke 17:15

"Thank you!" said Nana as the server set the pancakes on the table.

The server, Beverly, smiled and said, "You're welcome" before walking to the next table.

Nana asked Allie, "Will you thank God for our food?"

Allie smiled and said, "Nana, I see that people eat without thanking God. Do you think Jesus smiles like Miss Beverly does when we say thank You to Him?"

"Yes, Allie. I do," said Nana.

**Dear God,
Thank You for
everything You
have given me!**

Creator of All

In the beginning God created the heavens and the earth. Genesis 1:1

Last summer our family visited Kennedy Space Center. We loved the Hubble Space Telescope exhibits. This telescope takes pictures of planets and stars. As I watched the movie about space and faraway planets, I worshiped God, who created it all.

I do not have to look at pictures of faraway planets to remind me of God. At night, standing on my deck, all I have to do is look up. Through His creation, God constantly reminds me He is the Creator.

**Dear God,
Everywhere I look,
I am reminded that
You are the Creator
of everything.**

God's Very Good Creation

So God created man in his own image; he created him in the image of God; he created them male and female. Genesis 1:27

"This amusement park is amazing!" said Chloe to her dad.

"You made a friend when you gave the girl in line one of your bracelets," Dad said.

"While we were waiting, I tried to understand what her family was saying. I realized that we may sound different, but God created them too. God wants me to show love to everyone."

Dear God, Help me love others!

Love!

This is what I command you: Love one another. *John 15:17*

A person's last words can be important. The last words my grandmother said were: "Love one another." Because she lived her life loving others, I have a good example to follow. I think about how she treated people with kindness. She forgave easily. She put others first.

Just before Jesus died, He commanded His followers to love one another. He knew He would be beaten and killed. Still, Jesus loved everyone. His life is the greatest example.

**Dear God,
Thank You for
loving me! Please
help me love others!**

Love by Obeying

If you love me, you will keep my commands. John 14:15

Before Jesus returned to heaven, He told His disciples He would send the Holy Spirit. In that way, they would always be together. The Holy Spirit came to help them obey. By obeying Jesus, they showed Him their love.

We all need help obeying Jesus' commands. What commands are hard for you to obey? Is it difficult to show kindness to people who are unkind? Is it difficult to tell the truth? If you love Jesus, you can ask Him to help you obey.

**Dear God,
Please help me
show You love by
obeying You.**

No Distractions

Be careful to do as the Lord your God has commanded you; you are not to turn aside to the right or the left. *Deuteronomy 5:32*

Aaron and Randy ran to Aaron's mom. She said, "Go next door to Randy's house right away. His mom is waiting for you both."

"Okay," answered Aaron. "Come on, Randy."

Randy said, "Can we stop to look at the new kittens? It will not take long."

"Mom said to go to your house right away," Aaron said. "We can ask your mom later if we can see the kittens. Then we have not disobeyed Mom."

It is good the boys obeyed. God wants you to obey Him too.

**Dear God,
Please help me
obey all of Your
commands.**

Super Hero

I am able to do all things through him
who strengthens me. *Philippians 4:13*

Jeremy's little brother shouted, "I am a super-hero. The Bible says so!" Tommy continued, "The Bible says God will make me strong, and I can do anything!"

"God can do anything. But the Bible means that God will help us do what He wants us to do. We might be able to stand up for someone in trouble or say no to doing wrong things," Jeremy said.

"Sounds like a superhero to me!" shouted Tommy.

**Dear God,
Thank You for
giving me strength
to obey You.**

139

God's Way

But He [Jesus] answered, "It is written: Man must not live on bread alone but on every word that comes from the mouth of God." *Matthew 4:4*

When I was young, my family planned what to do if we had a fire in our house. We talked about which door was closest to each room. We decided where to meet outside. We found the fire extinguishers.

God also has a plan. He has a special plan for you. The Bible teaches you how to follow God's plan.

God's plan is for you to learn from the Bible and to pray. God wants you to do your best. He wants you to obey your parents. What else might God want?

**Dear God,
Thank You for
caring enough to
make a plan for me.**

All Things

All things were created through him [Jesus]. *John 1:3*

"Look what I made, Gran!" called Pat.

"That looks great," Gran said. "What is it?"

Pat laughed. "It is not anything special. I just wanted to make something with these cool colors."

"Did you know that being creative is one way Jesus wants you to live? God is creative, and He made people to be creative. Just think about all the things God has created for us!" Gran exclaimed.

"I never thought about being creative as a way to follow Jesus," Pat said.

Gran added, "It is one of God's great gifts!"

**Dear God,
Help me use my
creativity for You.**

Tell Jesus

If we confess our sins, he is faithful and righteous to forgive us our sins and to cleanse us from all unrighteousness. *1 John 1:9*

Sin is choosing your own way instead of God's way. Any time you choose to disobey God, you are choosing your own way. Your sin keeps you apart from God. But God loved you so much that He sent Jesus to be your Savior. He forgives your sin.

The plan only works when you are sorry for sinning. Then you can ask to be forgiven. When you ask, God forgives!

Dear God,
Thank You for
forgiving my sins.

Made Happy by God

He [Jesus] said, "It is more blessed to give than to receive." *Acts 20:35*

Katy's mom handed a bag of clothes to Mrs. Allen. Katy handed a box of toys to Anna. Mrs. Allen and Anna smiled. "Thank you so much!"

Later Katy said, "When you asked me to clean out my toy closet, I was a little angry. I wanted to keep everything!"

"How do you feel now?" asked Mom.

"The Allens were so happy to get these things. Making them happy makes me happy," Katy answered. "Do you think we could give away more of our things?"

"Absolutely!" Mom responded.

**Dear God,
Please help me give
happily to others.**

Belief and Trust

He [God] would . . . declare righteous the one who has faith in Jesus. *Romans 3:26*

Angelo asked his uncle Thomas, "What does the word *faith* mean?"

Thomas answered, "*Faith* is having trust in a person or thing. *Faith in Jesus* means believing and trusting in Him."

"I believe Jesus really lived," Angelo said.

"Faith is more than that. Faith in Jesus means you believe that Jesus is God's Son and the Savior. It means you believe Jesus died to pay the penalty for your sins," said Thomas.

"I believe those things!" said Angelo.

"Then you have faith!" answered Thomas.

**Dear God,
Help my faith
grow stronger.**

True Peace

Since we have been declared righteous
by faith, we have peace with God through
our Lord Jesus Christ. *Romans 5:1*

People have many symbols of peace. A dove or a white flag can be used to mean someone wants peace with an enemy. But what is peace? Your mom might mean she wants quiet. The president of a country might want a war to stop.

Peace with God means Jesus has taken your sins. When Jesus takes your sin, it no longer separates you from God. That is true peace.

**Dear God,
Thank You for peace.**

God Among Us

He [Joshua] said: "You will know that the living God is among you." *Joshua 3:10*

"Connie, how do you feel knowing God is always with us?" Candy asked her twin sister.

"It makes me feel good," said Connie.

"Thinking about God seeing me all the time and knowing what I do makes me feel safe," said Candy.

"I know God is always good. Knowing that He is with me makes me feel protected and loved," Connie said.

**Dear God,
I'm so glad You
love me enough
to be with me.**

Many People, One Body

We who are many are one body in Christ. Romans 12:5

"I love our church," said Sarah.

"I do too. I like to see people working together even though they have different talents. Mrs. Adams plays the piano. Mr. Sweet greets everyone at the door. Dad teaches your class," said Mom.

"God gives different people special things they are good at doing. That way our church can work together—just like our body works together," said Dad.

**Dear God,
Thank You for Your
plan to use everyone
in Your church.**

Sincerely Yours

Fear the Lord and worship him in sincerity and truth. *Joshua 24:14*

Daniel prayed his bedtime prayer but was still thinking about TV.

Uncle Mike asked, "Did you pray for your cousin to have a safe trip?"

Daniel said, "I do not remember. I was not paying attention."

Uncle Mike said, "Prayer is talking to the most important person of all—God. God wants you to pay attention when you talk to Him"

"I should pray again," Daniel said.

**Dear God,
Help me mean what
I say when I pray.**

148

Listen and Learn

Gather the people . . . so that they may listen and learn to fear the LORD your God and be careful to follow all the words of this law. *Deuteronomy 31:12*

"Every time I come over to your house, you are going to church. Why do you go to church anyway?" asked Whitney.

"God wants people who believe in Him to get together. He wants us to listen at church. He wants us to learn what He wants us to do. Can you come to church with us tomorrow? You can see for yourself why we go!"

Dear God
Help me to listen
and to learn.

WWJD?

The life I now live in the body, I live by faith in the Son of God, who loved me and gave himself for me. Galatians 2:20

"Kayla, why do you have WWJD on your bracelet?" asked Ann Marie.

"It stands for *What Would Jesus Do?* It reminds me to act like Jesus would," Kayla answered.

"How do you know what He would do?" asked Ann Marie.

"I know from the Bible how Jesus lived. He treated people with love and kindness. That helps me know how He wants me to live," said Kayla.

"Where can I get one of those bracelets?" Ann Marie asked.

**Dear God,
Help me live as
Jesus lived.**

God Works

Then Deborah said to Barak, "Go! This is the day the L<small>ORD</small> has handed Sisera over to you. Hasn't the L<small>ORD</small> gone before you?" *Judges 4:14*

Stephen saw his dog run into Mrs. Wilson's yard and break her flower pot. Stephen groaned.

Stephen prayed, *God, I know I must tell Mrs. Wilson what happened. It was an accident. Please help her understand and not be angry.*

Stephen rang Mrs. Wilson's doorbell. When she answered Stephen told her what happened.

"I saw the whole thing," she said with a smile. "Let's see if we can fix that pot."

Stephen knew then that God had answered his prayer.

**Dear God,
Please help me
remember that You
can do anything.**

The Love of God

All the LORD's ways show faithful love and
truth to those who keep his covenant
and decrees. *Psalm 25:10*

When Paige didn't clean up her toys when her parents asked her to, she had to sit in time out. When Chad argued with his little brother, he had to go to bed early.

When you do not obey your parents, they may punish you. They want you to learn how to act.

When Paige put all her books back on the bookshelf, Dad gave her a big hug. When Chad helped his mom cook supper, he was praised for helping.

God is always the One in charge. When people obey Him, they are doing what He asks them to do.

**Dear God,
Help me see Your
love and truth.**

What a Party!

There is joy in the presence of God's angels over one sinner who repents. Luke 15:10

We can't wait for summer. The July 4th celebration at Uncle Ron's house is always fun. We will have hot dogs, hamburgers, and cold drinks. Best of all, there will be rockets, smoke balls, and sparklers. What an exciting party!

When you repent (turn away) from your sin and ask Jesus to be your Lord (ruler or master), there is a party too! Jesus said that the angels in heaven celebrate when someone becomes part of God's family.

Dear God,
I'm happy that
You are glad when
people repent.

God Is Everywhere

Haven't I commanded you: be strong and courageous? Do not be afraid or discouraged, for the LORD your God is with you wherever you go. *Joshua 1:9*

One day at the fair, I rode a roller coaster. It went fast. It made me bounce in my seat. I was afraid. I knew God was with me. I could not see Him, but He was there. I prayed and told God I was afraid. He helped me remember to be strong and courageous. He wants you to be brave too. God is always with you.

**Dear God,
Help me know You
are always with me.**

Choose God's Way

God is my strong refuge; he makes
my way perfect. *2 Samuel 22:33*

Everyone must make choices. Sometimes it is hard
to make a choice. Knowing the right thing to do can
be hard. Often, both choices seem right. How can
you know what to do?

Read the Bible. Talk to God. He tells you His perfect way. God's way is the best way; it is the right
choice. Choose God's way.

**Dear God,
Help me always
choose Your way.**

God Always Listens

God is gracious to all who seek him. Ezra 8:22

Tess wanted to talk. She went to Mom. Mom was on the phone. Tess found Dad. He was mowing the grass. She even went to her brother to talk. He was busy playing a video game.

Tess remembered someone who would always listen. She prayed to God. God is never too busy to listen. Talk to God today.

Dear God,
Thank You for never
being too busy
to listen to me.

God Is Love

The one who does not love does not know God, because God is love. *1 John 4:8*

Kelli sat alone at a table. She looked sad.

Tina sat by Kelli. "What's wrong?" asked Tina.

"I forgot my lunch," Kelli said.

"I'll share mine. Take half of my sandwich," said Tina.

Tina cared about Kelli. She showed Kelli God's love by sharing her lunch. When you love God, you love other people. He loves them. God is love.

**Dear God,
Remind me to love
other people.**

God Is Always Right

God is a righteous judge and a God who shows his wrath every day. *Psalm 7:11*

"Jump!" shouted Jake.

Tony was standing on a tall ledge. He might get hurt.

"Do not jump," said Matt, Tony's older brother.

Tony trusted Matt. Tony knew Matt loved him.

You can trust God. He loves you. He gives you rules He wants you to obey. God's rules are always right. God's rules are always best.

**Dear God,
Help me to follow
Your rules.**

God Will Help

God is our refuge and strength, a helper who is always found in times of trouble. *Psalm 46:1*

You can ask God for help at any time. God is never too busy to help you. He is always with you when . . .

- You are drawing a picture.
- You are playing with friends.
- You are going to the store.
- You are alone.

**Dear God,
Help me remember
that You are
always with me.**

All the Time

This I know: God is for me. *Psalm 56:9*

God loves you. He will never stop loving you.

He loves you when you are happy. He loves you at church. He loves you in the daytime. He loves you when you are cranky. He loves you when you are sad. He loves you at home. He loves you at night. He loves you when you sing. You cannot do anything to make God stop loving you. God is love.

**Dear God,
Thank You for
loving me at
all times, no
matter what.**

Feelings

The LORD is gracious and righteous; our God is compassionate. *Psalm 116:5*

Happy	Sad	Angry
Excited	Bored	Sleepy
Hungry	Tired	Worried
Calm	Lonely	Grumpy

How are you feeling right now? There are many ways to feel. Feelings aren't wrong. It's okay to feel sad or angry sometimes. Tell God how you feel. He loves you.

**Dear God,
Today I feel**

_____.

161

All I Need

The LORD God planted a garden in Eden, . . . and there he placed the man he had formed. *Genesis 2:8*

God created the Garden of Eden for Adam and Eve. This special place had everything they needed.

God created a place for you to live as well! Everything you have comes from Him. Have you thanked God today?

Dear God,
Thank You
for giving me
everything I need.

Be Like God!

God said, "Let us make man in our image, according to our likeness." *Genesis 1:26*

God created all people. He created people to be different. Some people are short. Some people are tall. Some people have blue eyes. Some people have brown eyes. Some people have green eyes. Some people have curly hair. Some people have straight hair.

Even though we are different, God created all people to be like Him. God loves people. You can love people too. God does good things. You can choose to do good things too.

Dear God,
I want to be like You.

All Good!

God saw all that he had made, and it was very good. *Genesis 1:31*

God created the world in just six days. God made the light. He made the sky. He made the oceans and land. He made plants. He made the sun, moon, and stars. He made animals and people. God said that everything He had made was good. God still makes good things. He made your family and your friends. He even made you! Everything God makes is good.

**Dear God,
Thank You for
making so many
good things.**

Good Things

Everything created by God is good, and nothing is to be rejected if it is received with thanksgiving. 1 Timothy 4:4

You can be thankful God created a world full of good things. Thank God for creating your family. Thank God for creating your friends. Thank God for creating animals. Thank God for creating you! All that God created is good. What a wonderful God He is!

**Dear God,
Thank You for
creating a world
full of good things.**

Obey

Obey the L<small>ORD</small> your God and follow his commands and statutes. Deuteronomy 27:10

God gave rules to Adam and Eve. He wanted them to obey. God has rules for you too.

God's rules will help you be safe and happy.

Dear God,
Help me obey
Your rules.

God Can Help!

Our help is in the name of the LORD, the Maker of heaven and earth. *Psalm 124:8*

"Have you ever asked God for help?" asked Molly.

"I asked God to help my family stay safe when it was stormy," said Sarah.

"I have prayed that kind of prayer before. But I have a really big problem," said Molly.

"No problem is too big for God," said Sarah. "God had the power to create the world. Nothing is too hard for Him."

**Dear God,
Thank You for
caring about me
and my problems.**

167

Good Deeds

We are his workmanship, created in Christ Jesus for good works, which God prepared ahead of time for us to do. *Ephesians 2:10*

Jesus did good deeds. He was kind to people. He listened to people. He helped people who were sick. Jesus is our example for doing good deeds.

You can do good deeds too. The Bible tells you to love others. You can be kind to people. You can help people. You can share what you have. You can do what Jesus did!

**Dear God,
Help me do good
deeds so people
will know You.**

168

Worthy of Praise

Our Lord and God, you are worthy to receive glory and honor and power, because you have created all things, and by your will they exist and were created. *Revelation 4:11*

You can praise God. He is the Creator of the earth and every living thing. He created the sun, moon, and stars. He created the oceans and rivers. He created all things.

God is worthy of your praise!

**Dear God,
I praise You because
You are the Creator
of everything.**

169

Worship God Only

Fear the LORD and worship him in sincerity and truth. Joshua 24:14

You worship God when you spend time with Him. You worship God when you show honor to Him. Worship God by reading your Bible. Worship God by singing songs of praise to Him. Worship God by praying. Worship God at church. Worship God at home.

You can worship God anywhere. God wants you to worship Him only.

Dear God,
Thank You that
I can worship
You anywhere.

Why Go?

Come, let us worship and bow down. *Psalm 95:6*

Going to church is important. God wants you to worship Him. *Worship* is an action or feeling showing your love, praise, and respect for God. You can worship God by . . .

- Singing
- Giving money to the church
- Praying
- Listening to the pastor preach
- Reading your Bible

Dear God,
Help me know
that worshiping
You is important.

Sing, Sing, Sing

I will sing and make music to the LORD. Psalm 27:6

Tammy likes the music at church. It makes her happy. She likes the words about God's love. Tammy wishes everyone would sing. Some of her friends do not like to sing. Tammy learned in Sunday school that singing is one way to worship God. Tammy will tell her friends that they are worshiping God when they sing. Maybe then her friends will sing and be happy.

**Dear God,
Thank You for
giving us music.**

Serving God

Serve the Lord with gladness. Psalm 100:2

Have you ever helped serve your mom or dad breakfast in bed? To *serve* is to help or wait on someone. Sometimes children do that on Mother's or Father's Day. Serving your parents shows them you love them.

God wants you to serve Him. Going to church is one way you can serve God. It is also a way to honor Him. You are showing that God is important to you by going to church.

**Dear God,
Help me serve You
every Sunday!**

My Offering

He also saw a poor widow dropping in two tiny coins. Luke 21:2

God can do anything. He doesn't need your help. But God wants your help! He wants you to be part of His plans.

Giving money to your church helps make God's plans happen. Even a small amount can help needy families. Your money can also help support missionaries in other countries. Churches can use people's money to do great things.

**Dear God,
Thank You for
giving me ways
I can be part
of Your plan!**

Telling People

Go . . . and make disciples of all nations. Matthew 28:19

Telling others about Jesus is one of the most important things you can do! You and your church can tell people together. Can you think of some ways to tell?

- Invite a friend to go to church with you.
- Help your mother make cookies. Then take some of the cookies to a neighbor.
- Offer to take an older neighbor's mail to her.
- Offer to walk a neighbor's dog.

**Dear God,
Help me think
of ways to tell
people about You.**

Loving Others

Serve one another through love. Galatians 5:13

The people in Matt's church like to help people. They make shoebox gifts for children. Matt knows some children will not have a Christmas present without these gifts. The people at his church enjoy shopping for special gifts. The gifts are placed in the shoeboxes. Matt is pleased knowing these gifts will make children happy. Matt knows that his church loves other people.

**Dear God,
Thank You that
my church shows
love to people by
helping them!**

Pray for Others

Peter was kept in prison, but the church was praying fervently to God for him. Acts 12:5

The book of Acts tells a lot of stories about Peter. Peter loved God and told people about Him. The king did not like what Peter was preaching. The king had Peter thrown into jail.

The Bible says other people prayed for Peter. God heard those prayers. He sent an angel to help Peter escape from jail. Praying for others is what God wants you to do.

You can pray anywhere and at any time.

Dear God,
I want to pray for
others. Help me pray
for other people.

Love Each Other

By this everyone will know that you are my disciples, if you love one another. *John 13:35*

Sandy noticed that everyone at church was friendly. This was Sandy's first time to come to church. Her friend Beth invited her. Sandy saw people speak to each other. People gave each other hugs. People gave her hugs! Older people were helped up the stairs. Sandy liked all she saw. She knew the people at this church cared for each other.

Dear God, Thank You for my church and the care they show others.

The Blue Dress

Share with the saints in their needs. *Romans 12:13*

When I was in fourth grade, I gave my friend Amanda the clothes I had outgrown. She was happy to have them. On Sunday, Amanda wore my favorite blue dress. I'm not sure if her family was poor or not. But Amanda liked the clothes.

A Christian should be ready to help when people in his or her church have needs. You can help by sharing your clothes, food, and toys with people who need them.

Dear God,
Thank You for a
church that helps
each other.

179

With a Smile

Each person should do as he has decided in his heart—not reluctantly or out of compulsion, since God loves a cheerful giver. *2 Corinthians 9:7*

Did you know that even cows have best friends? God made you and me to receive love and give love. However, we often do nice things because we want something in return. God wants us to give because we want to give.

**Dear God,
Help me give
because I want
to give, not
because I feel like
I have to give.**

180

Fill in the Blank

What words would you use to describe summer? You might use some of these words: time with friends, adventure, sunny, relaxing, fun, and happiness.

What words would you use to describe God? You might use some of these words: awesome, King, Judge, loving, kind, gracious, giving, and helpful. Understanding God begins by knowing who He is and how BIG He really is. God is _____. I'll let you fill in the blank.

**Dear God,
Thank You for
creating everything
and being bigger
than everything.**

Choosing Jesus

He [Jesus] is Lord of all. *Acts 10:36*

You have choices to make. You can choose to learn the truths in the Bible. You can choose to believe Jesus died to forgive you of your sins. You can ask Jesus to be the Lord of your life. What does that mean?

Jesus loves you and knows what is best for you. You can choose to do things His way instead of your own way. Obeying Jesus shows how much you love Him.

**Dear God,
I choose Jesus as my
Savior and Lord.**

182

Number One

Exalt the LORD our God; bow in worship at his footstool. He is holy. Psalm 99:5

What do you like about summer? You can make a list, if you want. Now try making a list of everything you like or know about God. For as awesome as summer can be, God is so much more incredible. Keeping God as the number one best thing in your life is important.

**Dear God,
Help me keep You
number one every
day of my life.**

Life GPS

I will instruct you and show you the way to go; with my eye on you, I will give counsel. Psalm 32:8

Have you ever heard of a GPS? A GPS device can give you directions to where you want to go.

When it comes to living your life, God has given you the Bible to help you choose the right way to go. Doing what God's Word tells you to do is like doing what the voice from a GPS device tells you to do. God will never steer you wrong.

**Dear God,
Thank You for
giving me direction
in life. Help me
always do what
You tell me to do.**

Love When We Don't Deserve It

I knew that you are a gracious and compassionate God, slow to anger, abounding in faithful love. Jonah 4:2

God told Jonah to tell some evil people that He wanted to save them. Jonah became angry because he didn't think the people deserved to be saved.

Do you get angry at bad people? God wants to change the hearts of evil people. He is patient and good to all of us, even though we don't deserve His love.

**Dear God,
Thank You for
loving all people.**

185

The Greatest of All

LORD there is no one like you. You
are great. *Jeremiah 10:6*

On Independence Day, we celebrate the wonderful
country God has given us. On that night, people all
around can look up to see fireworks explode into
beautiful colors.

What is your favorite thing to see in the sky?
Fireworks? A rainbow? Clouds? When you look into
the sky, praise God for His greatness.

Dear God,
You are awesome,
beautiful, caring . . .

186

Just Call Out

I call on you in the day of my distress,
for you will answer me. *Psalm 86:7*

Daniel loved camping, but tonight he was afraid. A rock slide blocked their path home.

"Do you think anyone saw the flare, Dad?" Daniel asked.

"God heard our prayers before we sent up the flare," Dad assured Daniel.

When the ranger arrived, Daniel thanked God. God answers when you ask Him for help.

**Dear God,
Thank You for
hearing my prayers.**

His Eye on You

I will instruct you and show you the way to go; with my eye on you, I will give counsel. Psalm 32:8

Wandering through a maze can be fun unless you can't find your way out. Imagine your best friend guiding you out.

Jesus knows the answers to all of your problems. He keeps His eyes on you and is ready to guide you wherever you go.

**Dear God,
I am looking to
You to guide me.**

Think First

In all your ways know him, and he will make your paths straight. *Proverbs 3:6*

Dylan's baseball coach wouldn't let him play short-stop. On the way home, Dylan yelled, "I quit!"

"Dylan, you shouldn't decide that right now. First ask God what to do," Dad said.

Think about what God wants you to do before making a decision. He loves you and knows what is best.

Dear God,
Help me remember
to pray before I
make any decisions.

189

One Who Cares

Casting all your cares on him, because he cares about you. 1 Peter 5:7

At night, my granddaddy would lie on the couch with his legs dangling over the side. His Bible would be propped on his chest as he read. Finally he'd fall asleep. Granddaddy spent time telling God about his concerns. Then he'd rest, knowing God was taking care of him.

Talk with God about your concerns. Then relax in His care!

**Dear God,
Thank You for
caring for me.**

Even When It Is Difficult

Let those who suffer according to God's will entrust themselves to a faithful Creator while doing what is good. *1 Peter 4:19*

The man who wrote today's verse is one of my heroes. Peter tried to do good even when it was difficult. An evil king arrested Peter. Still Peter trusted Jesus. That night God sent an angel to set Peter free!

Dear God,
Help me trust You
and do good even
when it is difficult.

Pray and Obey

I call with all my heart; answer me, LORD. I will obey your statutes. Psalm 119:145

One morning my sons found something taped to the ceiling over their beds. I had secretly taped verses over Landon's and Kaden's beds to remind them to talk with God when they woke up.

If you could tape a verse on your ceiling, what would it say? Remember to talk with God. He will show you how to obey.

**Dear God,
Show me how
to obey You.**

192

Jesus Forgives!

Through this man [Jesus] forgiveness of sins
is being proclaimed to you. *Acts 13:38*

"Chloe, why are you crying?" Mom asked.

"I lied about your necklace. I lost it," Chloe confessed. "I'm so sorry, Mommy."

Mom hugged Chloe. "I forgive you, Chloe. Let's pray and tell Jesus how you feel. He will forgive you too."

When you do wrong, talk with Jesus. Ask Him to forgive you. He will make things right between God and you.

**Dear God,
Thank You for
Jesus, who
forgives my sins.**

Only God

Turn from these worthless things to the living God. Acts 14:15

Paul and Barnabas were upset! The people were worshiping make-believe gods.

The crowd wanted to worship Paul and Barnabas too. Paul and Barnabas shouted over the crowd, telling the people that God is the only true and living God. When you worship God, you help others know He is the only true God. Invite a friend to worship God with you.

**Dear God,
I worship only You.**

194

God Sees

Blessed are those who are persecuted
because of righteousness, for the kingdom
of heaven is theirs. *Matthew 5:10*

Not everyone chooses to follow the rules. Do you
know what happens to people who try to get away
with bad behavior? Most of the time they get caught!

God sees when you choose to follow the rules,
even if other kids aren't following the rules. Good
things will come to those who continue to follow
God's rules, even when others don't.

**Dear God,
Help me follow
You, even when
the people around
me don't.**

195

Good Witness

You will be a witness for him to all people of what you have seen and heard. *Acts 22:15*

After Jesus rose from the grave, His followers traveled everywhere they could, telling others about Jesus. They told others how Jesus had helped people and how He had healed people. They were sometimes teased. They were sometimes treated badly. Still, they kept telling others about Jesus. Being a good witness means telling others what you know about Jesus.

**Dear God,
Help me be a good
witness, telling
others about You.**

196

No Matter Where

About midnight Paul and Silas were praying and singing hymns to God, and the prisoners were listening to them. *Acts 16:25*

Do you sing or talk about God in places other than church? Paul and Silas did. They were followers of Jesus and were put in jail because of their faith in Jesus.

They kept praying and singing songs to God. They weren't afraid to praise God no matter where they were. Paul and Silas are a great example of how important it is to keep praising God no matter where you are.

Dear God,
Help me praise
You no matter
where I am.

Believe

They said, "Believe in the Lord Jesus,
and you will be saved." *Acts 16:31*

The word *believe* means to accept something as truth.

You sit in chairs, believing they will not break beneath you. You ride in cars, believing the drivers will safely get where you need to go.

Believing in Jesus means accepting what He says to be truth.

So the question is, "Do you really believe in Jesus?" He loves you and wants you to trust and accept Him as your Savior and Lord!

**Dear God,
Help me believe
in Jesus as my
Savior and Lord.**

198

Strong Enough

You, therefore, my son, be strong in the grace that is in Christ Jesus. 2 Timothy 2:1

Your body is growing and you're getting stronger every day. However, you may sometimes need help lifting heavy objects because your muscles aren't strong enough yet.

God can help you with all the difficult things you will face in life. By trusting Jesus as your Savior and Lord, you're given God's grace. You can't see or touch it. But God's grace is strong enough to help you no matter what.

**Dear God,
Thank You for
accepting me
as Your child.**

199

Big Words

When you send your breath, they are created, and you renew the surface of the ground. Psalm 104:30

God spoke and the world appeared. He breathed life into Adam. God's Word became flesh in the person of Jesus Christ.

Your words have power. The words you speak, the nice ones and the mean ones, affect others. Your words have the power to help people or hurt them. You can help make your world better by saying words God wants you to say.

**Dear God,
Thank You for
the power of
Your Word.**

Inspired

And whatever you do, in word or in deed, do everything in the name of the Lord Jesus, giving thanks to God the Father through him. Colossians 3:17

The word *inspire* means to fill someone with the urge or ability to do something.

Have you ever been inspired to play a sport, paint a picture, or sing a song? Who inspired you?

Jesus wants to inspire you too. He wants you to love God with your whole heart. Allow Jesus to inspire you to love God and love people.

Dear God,
Inspire me to be
who You created
me to be.

However

I will sing to the L ORD all my life; I will sing praise to my God while I live. *Psalm 104:33*

Do you like to sing? Whether you are an amazing singer or barely get the notes out, remember: God made your voice. He loves to hear you praise Him, and He loves to hear you join others in praising Him. Your voice is important because God made it. Use it so that everyone can hear about God's great love for us.

**Dear God,
Help me sing Your
praises every day.**

One Day

This same Jesus, who has been taken from you into heaven, will come in the same way that you have seen him going into heaven. Acts 1:11

Some people you love may live far away. Relatives may live far away. Friends may live far away. You may not see them all the time.

After rising from the grave, Jesus rose into heaven. But He'll be back one day to make sin go away forever. In the meantime, treat Jesus like the friend you love, knowing you'll see Him one day.

Dear God,
Thank You for the
promise of sending Jesus
back to us one day.

203

Only One God

Do not have other gods besides me. Exodus 20:3

This verse is the first commandment. God expects us to obey it. Before you think that this is an easy rule to follow, ask yourself these questions:

Would I rather learn about God or play a video game? Would I rather go to church or play soccer? Would I rather pray or eat a snack?

Video games, soccer, and snacks are not bad things, unless you love them more than you love God. Then they become gods.

**Dear God,
I love You more
than anyone or
anything else.**

No Idols

Do not make an idol for yourself. Exodus 20:4

What is your favorite thing to build with blocks? A tower? A house? A spaceship?

When my children were younger, I helped them build with Lego blocks. After we finished, we either saved what we built or took it apart to build something else. But we did not pretend it was a god and worship it.

Some people worship things, or idols, instead of God, but the Bible tells us to worship only God.

**Dear God,
I love You and
worship You only.**

He Is Holy

Do not misuse the name of the
L<small>ORD</small> your God. *Exodus 20:7*

On Sunday afternoons, my family rode through the countryside visiting neighbors. Whenever we stopped at Mr. Chester's farm, I wanted to cover my ears. He was loud and used a lot of words I wasn't allowed to say. One Sunday afternoon Mr. Chester greeted us with a smile. I was surprised. He looked different. He sounded different. He did not say one bad word. What happened?

My parents explained that Mr. Chester had trusted Jesus to forgive him of his sins. God had given him strength to make good choices.

**Dear God,
Help me to only
use Your name
with respect.**

Sunday: A Special Day

Remember the Sabbath day, to keep it holy. *Exodus 20:8*

"Why don't I go to preschool on Sundays?" Maria asked her mother.

"Because Sunday is a special day," Mother said. "God wants us to worship Him with other people and rest one day each week."

"Is that why we go to church on Sunday and then you take a nap in the afternoon?" Maria asked.

Mother laughed. "Yes, Maria, that's one way we show that Sunday is a special day."

**Dear God,
Please help me show
others that Sunday
is a special day.**

Honor Your Parents

Honor your father and your mother. Exodus 20:12

Telling your mother and father that you love them may be easy. But showing them you love them is not always easy. When you show your parents you love them, you are honoring them. Here are some ways you can honor your parents.

- Clean your room without fussing.
- Give your pet food and water.
- Hug your parents every day.
- Don't pout and cry when your parents tell you no.
- Be kind to your brother and sister.

**Dear God,
Help me show
my parents that
I love them.**

Show Love

Do not murder. *Exodus 20:13*

Wait! Slow down! Murdering or killing someone is something you will never do, so you may think you can skip today's devotion.

This command is in the Bible for everyone. Jesus says that when you think bad thoughts about other people, you break this rule.

God loves everyone, even people you are angry with. Pray and ask God to help you love people, even when you don't feel like loving them.

**Dear God,
Help me show
love to everyone
I meet today.**

Marriage Promise

Do not commit adultery. Exodus 20:14

Have you ever broken a promise you made to your parents, a friend, or a teacher? How did you feel?

When two people get married, they promise God that they will love one another and stay married forever. Sometimes mothers and daddies get mad, but they still love each other.

Adultery is when a husband and wife break their marriage promise. God forgives.

**Dear God,
Thank You for
Your love and
forgiveness.**

Stealing Is Wrong!

Do not steal. *Exodus 20:15*

Joel and Henry were playing video games at Henry's house. Henry's mom was in the kitchen when Henry saw his mom's purse on the sofa.

"Joel, when your mom takes us to the store on Saturday, let's buy a new game," Henry said.

"How will we pay for it?" Joel asked.

Joel saw Henry looking at his mom's purse. He reminded his friend that stealing is wrong.

Dear God,
Help me to
remember that
stealing is wrong.

211

Tell the Truth!

Do not give false testimony against
your neighbor. *Exodus 20:16*

Stella sat at her school desk. She was bored and
didn't want to finish her worksheet. Stella's best
friend Tonya sat next to her, so Stella began whispering to her friend.

Mrs. Morris was writing something on the marker
board when she heard someone giggling and talking. Mrs. Morris turned around and asked Stella if
she was talking instead of working. What do you
think Stella told Mrs. Morris?

**Dear God,
Please help me always
to tell the truth,
even when I might
get in trouble.**

Be Happy

Do not covet . . . anything that belongs to your neighbor. Exodus 20:17

The word *covet* means to want something that belongs to someone else. It is more than wishing for a new toy or video game. Coveting is wanting something so much that you will do anything to get it, even if that means disobeying God.

The Bible tells us this is wrong. God wants you to be happy with what He has already given you.

**Dear God,
Please help me be
happy with what
You have given me.**

Something from Nothing

In the beginning God created the heavens and the earth. *Genesis 1:1*

Have you ever used Play-Doh to make something? Maybe you made an animal, a plant, or a person. If you did not have any Play-Doh or other materials, could you still make something? No. But God can. To *create* means to make something out of nothing. God made the whole world out of nothing. He simply spoke, and it was. God is amazing! You can love and trust a God that powerful.

**Dear God,
You are powerful.
Help me trust You.**

God's Look–alike

So God created man in his own image; he created him in the image of God; he created them male and female. Genesis 1:27

"You look just like your dad." "You have the same smile as your mom." "Your eyes are blue just like your brother's eyes." Do people ever say things like this to you? It is cool how God made families look similar. The Bible says that you are created in God's image. This verse does not mean God has a body like ours. But we know things about Him by how He created us. God created you, so you know He loves you very much.

**Dear God,
Thank You for
making me in
Your image.**

He Hears You

I call on you, God, because you will answer me; listen closely to me; hear what I say. Psalm 17:6

"John? John? Can you hear me? I need your help. Why won't you answer me?" Katie was getting mad that her big brother would not answer her. Was he mad at her? Was he hiding from her so he would not have to help? She looked around the house for him. When she found him, she saw he had headphones on. He could not hear her. He was happy to help Katie when he knew she needed him.

Did you know that God always hears you? He will always answer you when you call Him. He is never too busy or too tired to help.

**Dear God,
I am so glad that You
always hear me.**

A Safe Place

Lord, You have been our refuge in every generation. Psalm 90:1

Carter's mom woke him up in the middle of the night. "Let's go, Carter. There is a bad storm. We must get to a safe place." Carter and his family went to a closet in the middle of their house. They waited until the storm was gone to come out.

Carter's family found refuge. A *refuge* is a safe place. The Bible says that when we are afraid or in trouble, we can go to God. He is our safe place. He loves you and will help you when you need Him.

**Dear God,
Help me find my
safe place in You.**

No Missing Pieces

So the heavens and the earth and everything in them were completed. *Genesis 2:1*

Lacey loved puzzles. She loved seeing all of the pieces come together to make one big picture. One day she had almost finished a puzzle when she saw that a piece was missing. Lacey was sad that she could not finish the picture.

When God created the world, He made it perfect. It was complete, not missing anything. Everything was exactly the way He wanted it to be.

**Dear God,
Thank You for Your
complete creation.**

Made for Joy

For everything was created by him, in heaven and on earth, . . . all things have been created through him and for him. Colossians 1:16

Jenny was so excited about her art project. It looked exactly the way she wanted it to look. She had so much fun making it. It brought her joy. She could not wait to show her mom and dad.

God created the whole world. He made everything we can see. He even made everything we cannot see. Why did God make everything? God's creation brings Him joy.

**Dear God,
Help me bring
You joy.**

Everywhere

Do not be afraid or discouraged, for the L*ORD* your God is with you wherever you go. *Joshua 1:9*

Maggie was nervous. Her family had just moved to a new city. She had to go to a new church. She had to make new friends. But Maggie remembered God's promise. He said He would be with her wherever she went. God would help her make friends. God would help her in her new church. She prayed, asking God to help her be brave. It did not take long for Maggie to love her new home.

**Dear God,
Thank You for
being with me
everywhere. Help
me be brave.**

220

Good Rest

God blessed the seventh day and
declared it holy, for on it he rested from
all his work of creation. *Genesis 2:3*

Creating the whole world must have been hard work. Do you think God was tired? No. The Bible says that God never gets tired. He is full of power. So why did He rest on the seventh day?

God was giving us an example to follow. He knew our bodies and minds would get tired. He showed us that rest is important. Some families rest on Sunday. Some families rest on Saturday. Some families rest on a different day. When and how does your family rest?

**Dear God,
Help me know when
and how to rest.**

One of a Kind

For us there is one God, the Father. All things are from him, and we exist for him. And there is one Lord, Jesus Christ. All things are through him, and we exist through him. 1 Corinthians 8:6

Toby collects baseball cards. He has a card that is one-of-a-kind. That means it is the only one like it. It is his favorite. It is special.

God is one-of-a-kind. There is no one like Him. He is special. No one else can do the things He does. No one else is as powerful. We would not be here without God. He is the Father who chose to create us and give us life. God made us to love Him.

**Dear God,
You are special.
I love You.**

222

Why Love?

I give you a new commandment: Love one another. Just as I have loved you, you are also to love one another. *John 13:34*

Think about the people in your life. Which people are easy to love? Why? Which people are hard to love? What makes them hard to love? It is hard to love someone who is mean to you. It is hard to love someone who is rude to you.

Jesus gave a command for you to follow. You are to love other people. What makes loving others easier is knowing that Jesus loved you first. Even when you make bad choices, Jesus still loves you. Knowing that, you can love those around you, even when it is difficult.

Dear God, Help me love others even when it is not easy.

Breath of Life

Then the LORD God formed the man out of
the dust from the ground and breathed the
breath of life into his nostrils, and the man
became a living being. *Genesis 2:7*

Eddie's dad drives an ambulance. He can help someone who has stopped breathing. When Eddie's dad
does CPR, he breathes air into someone's mouth. It
can save a person's life, but it does not create life.

God is more powerful than Eddie's dad. God
made the first man out of dirt. Then He breathed life
into the man. God's breath brought dirt to life and
made man. God is amazing!

**Dear God,
Thank You for the
life You give.**

Alive!

So it is written, The first man Adam became a living being. 1 Corinthians 15:45

Many movies and TV shows are about toys that come to life. The toys walk and talk and laugh and play. These stories are fun, but they are not real. Toys do not really come to life. Wouldn't it be fun if they could?

When God created the first man, He named him Adam. God shaped Adam out of dirt. Then the Bible says He breathed life into Adam. Adam came to life. This story really happened. God is powerful!

Dear God,
Because You are
powerful, I know
I can trust You.

225

Finding Help

I will instruct you and show you the way to go; with my eye on you, I will give counsel. Psalm 32:8

Mitchell had a problem. One of his friends was mad at him. Mitchell did not know why. He tried to solve the problem himself, but things only got worse. Mitchell decided to ask his dad for help. His dad was wise. His dad was happy to help him.

God knows everything. He sees everything. You can ask Him for help, just like Mitchell asked his dad for help. He promises to help you know what to do. And God is faithful. He keeps His promises.

**Dear God,
Guide me in the
way I should go.**

A Good Team

Then the LORD God said, "It is not good for the man to be alone. I will make a helper corresponding to him." *Genesis 2:18*

I like peanut butter sandwiches. But I love peanut butter and jelly sandwiches. Jelly makes the sandwich better. I like milk. But I love cookies and milk. Cookies make the milk better.

When God made man, He named him Adam. God did not want Adam to be alone. So He decided to make a helper for Adam. He did not give Adam just any helper. God gave man a helper who made him better. He made a woman and named her Eve. Adam and Eve were better together.

**Dear God,
Thank You
for making a
great team.**

227

The Perfect Man

The first man was from the earth, a man of dust; the second man is from heaven. 1 Corinthians 15:47

The first man God made was Adam. Adam was made out of dirt. Adam made a bad choice. Adam broke God's rules.

A long time after Adam, God sent Jesus to earth. God did not have to create Jesus. Jesus has always been. Jesus was in heaven with God. Jesus became a man too. Jesus never made a bad choice. He never broke God's rules. He was perfect.

Who do you think is better? Adam or Jesus? Who do you think is stronger? Adam or Jesus? Jesus! We can trust Jesus because He is perfect.

Dear God,
Thank You for Jesus.
Help me trust Him.

Heavy Problems

God is our refuge and strength, a helper who is always found in times of trouble. Psalm 46:1

Problems cannot always be seen with your eyes. They cannot be held in your hands. But when you have a problem, you might feel heavy. You might feel as if you were carrying around a heavy backpack. You might feel tired, sad, or afraid. You may not feel like you are strong enough to handle your problem.

When those times come, pray. Ask God to help you. God can be your safe place. He can be your strength. He promises to help you face your trouble.

**Dear God,
Help me turn to
You when I have
a problem.**

A Bad Choice

So the L<small>ORD</small> God sent him away from the garden of Eden to work the ground from which he was taken. Genesis 3:23

Adam and Eve made a bad choice. They disobeyed God. God is holy and perfect. Adam and Eve's bad choice separated them from their perfect God. God punished Adam and Eve for their bad choice. He made them leave the beautiful garden where they lived. God made Adam do hard work. But God never stopped loving Adam and Eve. He had a plan for them. He offered forgiveness.

**Dear God,
Thank You for Your love
and forgiveness when
I make bad choices.**

Showing Love

They exchanged the truth of God for a lie, and worshiped and served what has been created instead of the Creator, who is praised forever. Romans 1:25

God is our Creator. Tell Him you love Him. Sing songs to Him. Obey Him. Obey your parents.

Some people love the wrong things. They love things God made more than they love God. The Bible says these people believe a lie. They need to hear the truth. You can show them God's love by being kind. You can help them know whom to worship.

**Dear God,
I love You. Help
me show Your
love to others.**

231

The Highest

For the LORD, the Most High, is awe-inspiring, a great King over the whole earth. *Psalm 47:2*

Think of the greatest person you know. Think of the strongest person you know. Think of the most important person you know. Think of the wisest person you know.

God is greater than all of these people. He is stronger than anybody. He is powerful and wise. He is more than we can ever imagine. Nobody has ever been greater. And nobody will ever be greater. God is the best. And that amazing God loves you. You can trust Him.

**Dear God,
I am amazed
by Your love
and power.**

Hard Work

You will eat bread by the sweat of your brow until you return to the ground. Genesis 3:19

Have you ever grown a vegetable garden? It is difficult work. It will make you sweat. But it was not always that way.

Before Adam disobeyed God, his work in the garden was easy. After Adam disobeyed God, his work became difficult for the rest of his life. God punished Adam, but He never stopped loving him. God will never stop loving you.

**Dear God,
Thank You for loving
me even when I
choose to disobey.**

Remembering Jesus

The grace of God has appeared, bringing salvation for all people . . . while we wait for . . . Jesus Christ. *Titus 2:11–13*

Colby looked at the table in front of the church with the cups of juice and pieces of bread. He was excited he could celebrate the Lord's Supper as a Christian. He had learned the Lord's Supper is a special way to remember why Jesus died. Colby thought about Jesus dying to take the punishment for sin. He remembered the Bible teaching about Jesus rising from the dead. Colby knew Jesus had given him eternal life.

Dear God,
Thank You that
Jesus forgave
my sins.

Live Wisely

Teach me good judgment and discernment,
for I rely on your commands. *Psalm 119:66*

"Grandpa, will I be wise like you are when I am your age?" Ann asked.

Grandpa gave her a hug and said, "I can tell you how to become wise, even at your age. Remember these five words and you will have wisdom that pleases God: Do what the Bible says."

Ann repeated the words, "Do what the Bible says."

"So read the Bible and do what it says, and you will live wisely," Grandpa said.

**Dear God,
Teach me to
live wisely.**

235

Forever Love

I will sing about the LORD's faithful love forever; I will proclaim your faithfulness to all generations with my mouth. *Psalm 89:1*

Forever! That is a long time! Did you know that God promises He will love you forever? And God never breaks a promise. He is faithful. How does that make you feel? Happy? Thankful? Excited? If so, tell the people around you. Tell your family. Tell your friends. Tell your neighbors. Tell your teachers and coaches. Everyone needs to know about God's love and faithfulness.

Dear God,
Thank You for keeping
Your promises. Help
me tell people about
Your forever love.

236

Be Saved!

Adam said to his parents, "I feel like I have done something wrong. At Kid's Club, Mrs. Bell said if we are sorry for our sins and believe Jesus died to take our punishment, we can ask Him to forgive us." Adam thought for a minute and asked, "Can I ask God now?"

His parents said yes. Then they bowed their heads as Adam prayed.

Dear God,
I am sorry for my
sins. I trust Jesus to
forgive me. I want
to live for You.

Encouraged Every Day

For whatever was written in the past was written for our instruction, so that we may have hope. Romans 15:4

I loved visiting my grandmother. During the summer, I would run next door during the day to make sure she was not lonely. When she was sad, she read the Bible, and that encouraged her.

I learned that I could read the Bible and talk to God. When I rode my bike or did chores, I could think about God. You can read the Bible with your mom or dad and talk with God too.

**Dear God,
I like to talk to You.**

238

Only Jesus

I will never boast about anything except the cross of our Lord Jesus Christ. Galatians 6:14

How can you get to heaven? Some people brag about being good. But no one can be good enough to get to heaven. Just one sin separates a person from God. The Bible says everyone has sinned. God knew we could never be good enough, so He sent Jesus to die for our sins. When you trust Jesus to forgive you of your sins, God wipes away all of your sins. You can live with Him forever.

Dear God,
Thank You that I
can be with You in
heaven by becoming
a Christian!

Good News!

Believe the good news! *Mark 1:15*

I never get tired of hearing the good news that the Bible tells. When I am sad, the good news of Jesus cheers me up.

What is the good news? God loves you so much that He sent Jesus to make the way for you to live with Him forever. You can have a relationship with God beginning now. You can spend forever with Him in heaven. When you believe the good news of Jesus and trust Him with your life, you can find joy and strength to face any disappointments. Then you will want to tell others the good news too!

**Dear God,
I believe the good
news that Jesus
is the Savior!**

240

New Beginning

He said to me, "It is done! I am the Alpha and the Omega, the beginning and the end. I will freely give to the thirsty from the spring of the water of life." *Revelation 21:6*

Alpha is the first letter in the Greek alphabet. *Omega* is the last letter in the Greek alphabet. Jesus said, "I am the Alpha and the Omega, the Beginning and the End." Jesus can end all sin and give a new beginning. When you become a Christian, new life begins.

**Dear God,
Teach me about
my new life.**

Focus on Jesus

The peace of God, which surpasses all understanding, will guard your hearts and minds in Christ Jesus. *Philippians 4:7*

Jaden visited his grandpa in the hospital. "I came to cheer you up, Grandpa, but you already seem cheerful," said Jaden.

Grandpa patted his Bible that lay on the bed near him. "I have been thinking about Jesus," said Grandpa. "He is in control of my life. And I know He is with me now. He will be with me during my surgery too. So I just focus on Him."

Dear God,
Thank You for
giving me peace
when I focus
on Jesus.

No Worries

God is not a God of disorder but of peace. *1 Corinthians 14:33*

"Mom, will God always make sure we have food to eat?" asked Bailey.

"Yes, God will take care of our needs. We don't need to worry. We can trust God to take care of us," said Mom.

You can trust God too. You don't have to worry. Trust God to take care of you.

**Dear God,
Thank You for taking
care of all my needs.**

Alive!

In Christ all will be made alive. *1 Corinthians 15:22*

Fall is almost here. Soon the leaves will change colors and fall off the trees. The green grass will die. Many flowers die in the winter. But then comes spring! New leaves appear on the trees. New flowers and plants grow. God is making things come alive.

Jesus died. But He did not stay dead. After three days, God made Him alive! One day God will do the same thing for everyone who trusts Jesus. God will make them alive! Jesus made it possible.

**Dear God,
Thank You for
giving me life.**

Eyes on You

The LORD keeps his eye on those who fear him— those who depend on his faithful love. *Psalm 33:18*

Have you ever gone to check the mailbox by your-self? Or have you ever walked to a neighbor's house to play? Did your mom watch you to make sure you made it safely? Maybe you have played at the park while your dad watched from a park bench. Your parents keep their eyes on you. They watch you to keep you safe. Why? Because they love you.

God loves you even more than your parents do. He watches you. He protects you. He loves you with a love that never ends. You can depend on Him.

**Dear God,
Help me depend
on Your never-
ending love.**

245

Best Friends

Noah was a righteous man, blameless among his contemporaries; Noah walked with God. Genesis 6:9

Gracie loves her friend Ella. They spend a lot of time together. They are best friends. Do you have a best friend?

Noah had a best friend. His best friend was God. The Bible says that Noah "walked" with God. It does not mean that they walked down the road together. Noah could not see God. It means that Noah listened to God. Noah talked to God. God loved Noah.

Dear God,
Help me walk with
You every day.

Joy

The LORD values those who fear him, those who put their hope in his faithful love. *Psalm 147:11*

Jennie has a toy cat that meows. It is her favorite toy. She takes her toy cat everywhere. It makes her happy. Jennie values her cat. To *value* something means you think it is important and you enjoy it. Think of your favorite toy. Does it make you happy? If it makes you happy, you value that toy.

When you trust in God's love for you, you bring Him joy. When you love Him and obey His commands, you make Him happy. God values you. You are important to God. Praise Him!

**Dear God,
I can trust in Your
love for me. Thank
You for valuing me.**

247

Perfect Timing

When the time came to completion, God sent his Son, born of a woman. *Galatians 4:4*

Hudson was carrying a big stack of books to his room. The books got too heavy, and Hudson dropped them all over the floor. Right then, his brother walked in, helped Hudson pick up the books, and carried the heaviest books for Hudson. His brother came at the perfect time.

God's timing is always perfect. He sent Jesus to earth as a baby. He sent Jesus at exactly the right time. He sent Jesus to save the world. We can trust Him.

Dear God,
Thank You for Your
perfect timing.

248

All Mapped Out

For his faithful love to us is great; the LORD's faithfulness endures forever. Hallelujah! *Psalm 117:2*

Brady looked at the map in his hand and smiled. He didn't know what all the symbols on the map meant or where to start. Brady's dad knew exactly where to go because he had been there before.

"Dad, I am glad you are going with me. I am not afraid of getting lost, and I am really excited to see where we end up!" said Brady.

Brady's dad knew the best way to get to their destination. God knows the best route for your life. He will take you where He promised.

Dear God,
Thank You for
always keeping
Your promises!

249

A Promised "Yes"

For every one of God's promises is
"Yes" in him. *2 Corinthians 1:20*

"I would love to go to the park with you," said Jenny, "but I promised my mom I would finish putting away my toys first."

"It will not be a big deal," said Sarah. "You can clean up later."

"But then I would be disobeying my mom," said Jenny. "My parents told me that I should follow God's example all of the time. God always keeps His promises, so I want to keep my promises too."

"I guess you are right," said Sarah. "Hey! Maybe we can go to the park when you finish!"

**Dear God,
Help me keep
my promises.**

No Lie

Teach me good judgment and discernment,
for I rely on your commands. *Psalm 119:66*

"Adam asked me to let him copy my homework,"
said Brittany. "I do not want him to be mad at me."

"God gives commands that teach you how to
live," said Mom. "Look at what He has to say."

As they read the Bible, Brittany discovered that
God said a lot about not telling the truth—that it is
wrong. So she prayed and asked God to help her
tell Adam her decision. Letting him copy her homework would not be telling the truth, and she wanted
to do what was right.

**Dear God,
Help me know Your
commands so I can make
the right decisions.**

The Rain and the Flood

The bow will be in the clouds, and I will look at it and remember the permanent covenant between God and all the living creatures on earth. Genesis 9:16

God asked Noah to build an ark, and on it to put his family and pairs of every kind of animal. Noah obeyed. Then God sent a flood to wipe out every living creature. Noah, his family, and the animals were safe. The rain stopped. The flood waters dried up. Then God sent a rainbow as a symbol of His promise to never again destroy the earth with a flood.

**Dear God,
Help others know
Your promises.**

Love in Action

I rejoice over your promise like one who finds vast treasure. Psalm 119:162

Jesus loved people. He healed people. Jesus knew what God's promise of forgiveness would mean to people. Jesus spoke about God's commands. People listened to what He had to say.

You can serve and help people! When you do, people see Jesus' love in action. And you can tell them about God's promise too!

**Dear God,
Help me help others
and show them Your
love in action!**

253

Serve It Up

Serve the LORD with gladness; come before him with joyful songs. Psalm 100:2

"Mom, I love singing in the children's choir," said Anna. "I like helping people worship when I sing. What is another way I can help?"

"After the worship service, pick up the worship folders from the pews and take them to the door. Worshipers can use those in the second service," said Mom.

"I am glad I can serve God doing that too!" said Anna.

**Dear God,
Thank You that I
can serve You.**

After His Heart

For your faithful love guides me, and
I live by your truth. *Psalm 26:3*

King David was called a man after God's own heart. David loved, honored, and followed God with everything he did. David wrote today's psalm about how wonderful God is and that He deserves to be praised.

You can help other people know God too. You can tell them about His love and all that He's done for you.

Dear God,
Thank You for teaching
me about Your love
through the Bible.

God Remembered

God remembered Noah, as well as all the wildlife and all the livestock that were with him in the ark. Genesis 8:1

God took care of Noah and all the creatures with him on the ark. Jesus cared for people and animals too. Jesus is the best example for how to live honoring God. You can honor God by treating everything and every creature with kindness.

Dear God,
Thank You for
caring for me.
Help me care for
others also.

A Plan to Stay

"For I know the plans I have for you"—this is the LORD's declaration. *Jeremiah 29:11*

"Mom, why did Missy have to move all the way to Mexico?" asked Jenna.

"Missy's mom and dad decided to become missionaries," said Mom. "They are going to live in Mexico and teach people about Jesus."

"They couldn't do that here?" whined Jenna.

Mom laughed. "Yes, of course, but God wants them in Mexico right now. You both get to help others know Jesus, just in different countries. I know you will miss her, but God has a plan for Missy and for you."

**Dear God,
Thank You for
having a special
plan for my life.**

A Crazy Mess

The whole earth had the same language and vocabulary. Genesis 11:1

Did you know everyone used to speak the same language? But people started making plans that were not God's plans. The people built a tall tower so other people would hear about their plans. God created different languages to turn the people back to Him and His plan. The city and tower were never finished because the people could not understand each other.

When you do not obey God, life gets messy. And most of the time, you are not the only one who gets caught in the mess. Learn God's commands and obey them.

**Dear God,
Teach me to obey
Your commands.**

258

Grace Gives

I commit you to God and to the word of his grace, which is able to build you up. *Acts 20:32*

"Jesus taught about God's grace," said Mr. Black. "*Grace* means that God gave us a gift we did not deserve."

"Kind of like being nice to a kid who is mean to me?" asked Renee.

Mr. Black smiled. "Jesus died on a cross for your sins so you could trust Him and receive God's gift of eternal life," explained Mr. Black. "And He asks you to make sure other people hear about Him so they can have that chance too."

Dear God,
Show me how to
help others know
Your grace.

259

Trusting the Plan

I know that you can do anything and no plan of yours can be thwarted. *Job 42:2*

God created the whole universe and everyone in it. God sends the rain and makes the sun shine. God also sent His only Son to die for your sins.

God can do anything, and He loves You so much that He has a special plan for your life. Nothing and no one can change God's plan. You can trust that He will show you that plan and how to help others know Him.

**Dear God,
Help me know and
trust in Your plan.**

260

Scattered

The LORD scattered them throughout the earth. *Genesis 11:9*

Do you remember reading about the Tower of Babylon? God's people built a big tower and city so others would know and respect them. But that is not what God wanted. God wanted them to honor and obey Him. God made them all speak different languages and sent them all to different places so they could not honor themselves so easily.

Disobedience always has consequences. The good news is God teaches you how to obey Him through His Word!

**Dear God,
Thank You for
teaching me how
to obey You.**

261

Agree with God

For in my inner self I delight in
God's law. *Romans 7:22*

Jesus lived and obeyed God's law perfectly. What a big change—coming from heaven to an earth full of sin! But Jesus did not just live and obey perfectly—He did it joyfully!

Jesus was our perfect example. So how do we live and obey God? Joyfully! And that loving attitude will show through to others as we help and serve them too!

**Dear God,
Help me serve You
and others with joy!**

262

Should I Be Scared?

So keep the commands of the Lord your God by walking in his ways and fearing him. Deuteronomy 8:6

"Mom, the Bible says to fear the Lord. Does that mean I should be scared of Him?" asked Jaden.

"No, it means that you need to respect God for who He is and what He does," said Mom.

"So I can give Him respect by knowing Him, doing what He says in the Bible, and following His plan for my life?" asked Jaden.

Mom smiled and said, "Exactly!"

**Dear God,
Help me keep
Your commands
as I follow Your
plan for my life.**

263

Choose to Help

I will bless those who bless you, I will curse anyone who treats you with contempt, and all the peoples on earth will be blessed through you. Genesis 12:3

God asked Abraham to take his family and all of his belongings and move to a faraway land. Because Abraham obeyed, God blessed him and his family forever!

When you choose to obey God, your choices can help other people know Him. Keep reading the Bible and doing what God says—even when it is not easy!

**Dear God,
Help me make
choices that lead
others to know You.**

Known

I will make your name great, and you
will be a blessing. *Genesis 12:2*

What does it mean to have a great name? Abraham's obedience to God made His name well known.

Jesus is also well known because of His obedience to God. Jesus died on a cross because God wanted you to have a chance to know Him. Think about how many people's lives were changed because Jesus obeyed.

Do you want to help others know God? Love them. Help them. Pray for them. And use different ways to tell them all about Jesus.

**Dear God,
Help me be known
for obeying You.**

A Recipe for Praise

May the name of God be praised forever and ever, for wisdom and power belong to him. *Daniel 2:20*

"Dad, what does it mean to praise God?" asked Mischa.

"You can praise God lots of different ways. You can sing, obey His word, pray, and tell others about all He has done for you," said Dad.

"I can praise God by telling Mrs. Sanders how much Jesus loves her," said Mischa.

"Right!" said Dad. "That sounds like a great idea!"

**Dear God,
I want to
praise You.**

Ask for Help

My tongue sings about your promise, for all your commands are righteous. *Psalm 119:172*

King David was not a perfect man, but he was wise. He wanted to please God by obeying His commands. He asked God to help him understand the commands.

God promises to teach you how to follow Him. He does that through the Bible. When you do not understand what you read, pray and ask Him to help you. As you learn new things from God's Word, you can teach others so they can learn and grow closer to God too!

Dear God,
Help me know
Your commands so
I can obey them.

Reflect Jesus

Christ also suffered for sins once for all, the righteous for the unrighteous, that he might bring you to God. *1 Peter 3:18*

Jesus did all that He did so you could know God. Jesus showed you how to live in the way He lived. He served others. He helped people to know God.

You can do that too! Pay attention to how Jesus treated people and treat them that way. If they need help with something, even washing windows or raking leaves, help them! With everything you do, let your attitude and your words reflect Jesus.

**Dear God,
Help me to help
others know
Jesus as I love
and serve them.**

Wherever I Go

My house will be called a house of prayer for all nations. Isaiah 56:7

God loves you and wants you to know Him, but He sent Jesus to die for the sins of all those who believe in Him. That is why He asks you to tell others about Him. Part of His plan is for you to show others His love and teach them His commands. You can talk about Jesus anywhere, not just at church! That way, more people can know God and become part of His family.

**Dear God,
Help me to help
others know You
wherever I go.**

269

Faith to Follow

Abram believed the LORD, and he credited it to him as righteousness. Genesis 15:6

God told Abram that He would one day have as many children and grandchildren as stars in the sky. Abram believed God. Abram had faith. Abram trusted God to do what He said.

God can do anything. Obey Him no matter how impossible or scary it may feel. Your faith may lead others to know God.

**Dear God,
Help me obey You
no matter what.**

270

Like Jesus

Your sins have been forgiven on account
of his [Jesus'] name. *1 John 2:12*

Jesus lived a perfect life and died for your sins.
Because of that, God will forgive you if you ask. It
does not matter what you have done or how much
you messed up in the past. God will forgive you
because of what Jesus did for you.

God asks you to love others too. That means forgiving them when they do something wrong. That
means being nice to people who are mean to you.
When you live like Jesus, you help other people
know God.

**Dear God,
Help me forgive
others and love
like Jesus.**

Always Show Love

Love the LORD your God with all your
heart, with all your soul, and with all
your strength. *Deuteronomy 6:5*

"Aunt Tina, sometimes it is really difficult to know
what God wants me to do," said Alison.

"God says the most important things are loving
Him and loving others," said Aunt Tina.

"What if I stop being Andre's friend because
Breanna does not like him? I guess I am not being
loving toward Andre or God," said Alison.

"Remember," said Aunt Tina, "being Andre's
friend might even help him know Jesus."

**Dear God,
Help me love
others like You
asked me to do.**

Love Is the Reward

For the word of God is . . . able to judge the thoughts and intentions of the heart. *Hebrews 4:12*

God always knows why you do what you do. Jesus lived the right way, and you can live by following His example. Jesus helped people because He wanted people to know God.

Helping people for the right reasons can be difficult. Instead of asking what you will get for obeying God or helping someone, ask how it will show God's love to everyone around you.

**Dear God,
Help me see how
my words and
actions can show
others Your love.**

God's Listening!

God has listened; he has paid attention to the sound of my prayer. *Psalm 66:19*

"Dad! I asked God to help me remember what I had learned for the belt test at my karate class. I came in second place!" said Trey.

"That is awesome, buddy!" said Dad. "God always hears our prayers."

Trey thought about his friend Kevin's sad look when he did not place at the karate test. "I think it would make God happy if I offered to help Kevin practice so he can place next time too," said Trey.

"That is a great idea," said Dad. "You have thought of a great way to show God's love."

**Dear God,
Help me show Your
love at all times.**

Drifting Together

Do everything in love. *1 Corinthians 16:14*

Did you know that sea otters hold hands while they sleep so they don't drift apart? It might look like love, but it's nothing compared to the love God has for you.

God is always there for you because He loves you. One way we can put God first is to be there for the people we care about too. Choosing to love people keeps you from drifting apart from them. This helps your love last.

**Dear God,
Help me do things
and help people
out of love, not just
when I feel like it.**

Starts with Me

Go, therefore, and make disciples of all nations, baptizing them in the name of the Father and of the Son and of the Holy Spirit. Matthew 28:19

Millions of trees are planted every year because squirrels forget where they put their nuts. These nuts, or seeds, grow into trees.

People hear about God when someone like you tells them about God's love. Planting this seed helps faith grow. You come to know Jesus, then you can tell people about Him! Someone's growing faith in Jesus might just start with you.

**Dear God,
Help me know You
and tell others
about You.**

Good Day

He lets me lie down in green pastures; he leads me beside quiet waters. Psalm 23:2

What a perfect day, Liz thought to herself. *I got to eat breakfast by the ocean. I got to sit by the pool all day. Now I'm sitting at the campfire with all my friends and family. What a great day!*

God wants to take care of you. He can't grow you unless you follow Him every day. Each day you allow God to guide you is a good day.

**Dear God,
Thank You for
guiding me. Help
me follow You
every day.**

And...

And remember, I am with you always, to the end of the age. *Matthew 28:20*

"I can't do it," Emma shouted in frustration. Emma had tried and tried to walk across the balance beam but kept falling off.

Emma's dad said, "Try it one more time. This time hold my hand." Emma held her dad's hand and walked the entire way without falling.

Some things in life seem easy. Some seem hard. No matter what, God's hand is already stretched out for you to hold.

Dear God,
Thank You for
always being
here for me, no
matter what.

Viewing Jesus

You will receive power when the Holy Spirit has
come on you, and you will be my witnesses
in Jerusalem, in all Judea and Samaria,
and to the end of the earth. *Acts 1:8*

When you see something cool or funny, you are a
witness of something cool or funny. You probably
want to tell other people about it. That's how videos
get millions of views on the Internet.

When the good news of Jesus is seen by others in
the way you live, you are a witness. God wants you
to help others see Jesus through the way you live.

**Dear God,
Help me be a witness
of Your great love.**

Learn from God's Word

Blessed are those who hear the word
of God and keep it. *Luke 11:28*

Dylan was happy. Owen was not. Dylan had saved the money he needed to buy what he wanted. Owen had heard about saving money, but instead he spent all of his money on stuff he didn't even have anymore.

Just hearing Bible stories won't change your life. You must listen to God's Word and learn from it. When you do this, God's Word can help you do what is right. God's Word can make you strong.

**Dear God,
Help me to learn
from Your Word.**

Choosing God's Way

Worship the Lord your God, and serve only him. *Matthew 4:10*

Penguins choose one mate and follow only that mate for life. Following God means putting what He says above everything else and doing what God says to do. Serving God means behaving the way He wants us to, no matter what. Choose to worship God, and your choices will follow Him.

Dear God,
Thank You for loving me. Help me read the Bible every day and follow You.

281

Closer Together

You planned evil against me; God planned it for good to bring about the present result— the survival of many people. Genesis 50:20

Sometimes bad things happen. So what do you do when things don't go the way you want? No matter what, you have God. He cares about you and your family. God can help in any situation. God wants you and your family to grow closer together, especially when something bad happens. Keep trusting God.

**Dear God,
Help me grow closer
to You and my family,
especially during
difficult times.**

Really Listen

All the people listened attentively to the
book of the law. *Nehemiah 8:3*

"Come on," Olivia called to Mia.

"Come on, where?" asked Mia.

"Weren't you listening?" Olivia continued. "Mom
just told us everything we need to do next."

"Oh," stated Mia. "I guess I wasn't listening."

Sometimes you may not listen when people talk
to you. The best way to learn God's Word is to listen. Are you listening? Really listening?

**Dear God,
Help me really
listen to You.**

283

Many Good Things

We eagerly wait through the Spirit, by faith, the hope of righteousness. *Galatians 5:5*

"I just can't wait any longer," Andrew blurted out. "I want to go to the zoo today!"

Have you ever been promised something that you had to wait for, maybe even wait a long time? Many good things come to those who follow God and believe in Jesus. Some good things come right away. Some come later. Keep trusting Jesus. God will continue to prove Himself faithful.

**Dear God,
Help me be patient
as I follow You
every day.**

Stay Clean

How can a young man keep his way pure?
By keeping your word. Psalm 119:9

What would happen if you never took a bath or brushed your teeth? We all get dirty. If we stay dirty, bad things happen to our bodies. You may not like taking baths or brushing your teeth every day, but it's so important.

Keeping your mind and heart clean is also very important. God forgives you of your sins when you ask Him. This verse says that your best plan to stay clean is to do what the Bible says.

Dear God,
Help me read the
Bible every day.

Healthy and Strong

Now may the God of hope fill you with all joy
and peace as you believe. *Romans 15:13*

Fill your body with healthy foods to help your body
stay well.

Fill your body with unhealthy foods, and you will
become sick. The same is true for your beliefs. Fill
your mind and heart with God's truth, every day. He
can keep you joyful, peaceful, and strong.

Dear God,
Help me fill my mind
and heart with Your
truth every day.

Run

Let the little children come to me. Don't stop them, because the kingdom of God belongs to such as these. Mark 10:14

How many times have you been told to stop running in the house? When kids started running toward Jesus, the disciples tried to stop them. Jesus told the kids that it was okay to run to Him. Jesus wants you to love Him so much that you want to run toward Him. When you do this, you'll never hear Jesus say, "Stop running!"

**Dear God,
Help me run toward
Jesus every day.**

Be Prepared

In your hearts regard Christ the Lord as holy, ready at any time to give a defense to anyone who asks you for a reason for the hope that is in you. *1 Peter 3:15*

Your parents make a lot of plans so that your family can live comfortably and do a lot of things. While you may make lots of plans in life, God wants you to be ready to tell people about His love and His Word. Be prepared to tell about God even if you did not plan to do so. You can learn to do this by reading your Bible, praying, and worshiping Him. How prepared are you?

**Dear God,
Help me be
prepared to tell
people I meet that
You love them.**

Never Broken

The LORD will fulfill his purpose for me. LORD, your faithful love endures forever. Psalm 138:8

"It broke!" shouted Ryder.

"Well, I didn't break it," responded Alexa. "If we can't play on our swing set anymore, what do we do now?"

Things get broken all the time. Some items can be fixed. Some need to be thrown away. Sometimes people feel broken. They feel like they're not good enough, or they listen to the mean things people say. God doesn't want you to feel broken. Keep following Him.

**Dear God,
Thank You for
always loving me
and guiding me.**

Heaven's Song

Holy, holy, holy is the Lord of Armies; his glory fills the whole earth. Isaiah 6:3

What is your favorite song right now? Heaven has a favorite song. While we don't know the melody to it, we know that all of heaven sings to God, "Holy, holy, holy is the Lord of Armies; his glory fills the whole earth." While you may get tired of hearing the same song again and again, heaven never tires of singing God's praises.

**Dear God,
Help me praise Your
name every day.**

Father Knows Best

Don't be like them, because your Father knows the things you need before you ask him. *Matthew 6:8*

Have you ever lied to your parents to get something you wanted? Some people lie to God to get what they want. They say all the right words in front of people. Then they act differently when no one is looking. God sees and knows everything you do. He always knows what's best, and He wants to give you His best. He can't give you His best unless you trust Him enough to be honest.

**Dear God,
No matter what,
help me to always be
honest with You.**

Big Little Things

But his servants approached and said to him,
"My father, if the prophet had told you to do
some great thing, would you not have done it?
How much more should you do it when he only
tells you, 'Wash and be clean'?" *2 Kings 5:13*

God is the Lord of big things and little things. While
He could do everything Himself, He chooses to
include us in His story. Sometimes the most miraculous things are the things most people don't see.

Obey God with the little things. It will help your
life in big ways.

**Dear God,
Help me follow
You with both the
big things and the
little things.**

292

Worth Repeating

Haven't I commanded you: be strong and courageous? Do not be afraid or discouraged, for the LORD your God is with you wherever you go. Joshua 1:9

How many times have you heard the phrase "I love you" from your family and friends? Probably too many times to count? Some things are worth repeating. The phrase "be strong and courageous" is mentioned more than thirty times in the Bible. God tells you to be strong and courageous because He is always with you.

**Dear God,
Thank You for being
with me, especially
when I'm afraid.**

293

The Safest Place

I call on you in the day of my distress, for you will answer me. *Psalm 86:7*

Do you know where to go in your house if a big storm comes? We are taught what to do when danger comes. But what about the storms in life? The answer to every situation you will ever face, the good and the bad, is to run to God. He is, and always will be, the safest place.

**Dear God,
Thank You for
always being
here for me.**

In Return

The life I now live in the body, I live by faith in the Son of God, who loved me and gave himself for me. *Galatians 2:20*

Giving something without wanting anything in return is difficult. That is exactly what Jesus did. He gave everything for you. He sacrificed His life for you. What does that truth cause you to want to do for Him to show how thankful you are? One way you can give back to God is through loving others.

Dear God,
Help me honor You
and love others
every day.

Something Wonderful

*Be kind and compassionate to one another,
forgiving one another, just as God also
forgave you in Christ. Ephesians 4:32*

"It is not my fault!" shouted Jacob to his dad. "I just did what everyone else was doing. I did not know I would get in trouble."

When you get caught doing something you shouldn't, you may fail to say the one thing that really matters, "I am sorry!" Truly being sorry allows for something wonderful—forgiveness. God is ready to forgive you. He also wants you to forgive others.

**Dear God,
Thank You for
showing me what
true forgiveness is.**

296

Our Tour

I have given you an example, that you also should do just as I have done for you. John 13:15

Kelley was nervous. She had never tied her own shoes. Her mother calmly and confidently looked at her and said, "I have shown you how to do it. Now it is your turn!"

You started learning how to do new things when you were born, and you continue to learn. Some things you learn easily. Other things are harder for you to learn or do. Jesus gave you the best example ever for living a life of faith. Now it's your turn to help others know about Jesus.

**Dear God,
Help me tell people
about Jesus.**

Right On

Children, obey your parents in the Lord,
because this is right. *Ephesians 6:1*

Do you know what the word *right* means? *Right* means to act or speak in a way that agrees with the truth. The word *right* also means to be on the side of truth, justice, or goodness. Choosing to obey God and the people He tells you to trust, like your parents, helps you to be completely right!

**Dear God,
Thank You for
showing me the
right way to live.**

Call on God

LORD, hear my prayer; listen to my
plea for mercy. *Psalm 86:6*

The first phone number most kids learn is 9-1-1.
Why? Because 9-1-1 is the number you can call
from any phone when there is an emergency. Stories
are told of 3- and 4-year-olds calling 9-1-1 to save
people when bad things happened. You can call this
number anytime, any day or night, when you have
an emergency.

You can pray to God anytime and anywhere. God
hears every prayer, every time. God wants you to
talk to Him every day.

Dear God,
Thank You that I can
talk to You anytime
and for any reason.

All of You

Casting all your cares on him, because he cares about you. *1 Peter 5:7*

Brenna was scared. "A friend was mean to me at the park yesterday," she said to her brother.

"You should tell Dad," her brother said.

"But he's so busy. He has way more important things to do," said Brenna.

"Dad will always make time for you. You are more important to him than work!"

God is our Father. He cares about big things like earthquakes and wars. But He also cares about you! He wants you to trust Him with your whole life.

**Dear God,
Help me trust You
with my whole
life. Thank You
for loving me.**

Good Fruit

Even a young man is known by his actions—by whether his behavior is pure and upright. *Proverbs 20:11*

Your words and actions come from what you see and hear. If you watch and listen to good things, you will probably say and do good things. The best way to keep your behavior pure and upright is to read your Bible and learn how God wants you to live, all the time.

**Dear God,
Help me keep Jesus
close to me.**

Everything You Need

The LORD is my shepherd; I have what I need. *Psalm 23:1*

A farmer has a tough job that never ends. He plants, waters, and harvests crops at just the right time. He feeds, waters, and provides shelter for animals that could not survive without him. A farm without a farmer will not grow much food.

God's love is similar to a farmer's love. God knows there is a lot in life that can make you sad. When you allow Him, God will care for you and provide for you. He can give you what you need to live a life that honors Him.

**Dear God,
I trust You with
everything
in my life.**

Strong and Courageous

Do not be afraid or discouraged, for the LORD your God is with you wherever you go. Joshua 1:9

To do some jobs a person must show courage. Courage is doing what needs to be done when you are afraid. Courage is following what God wants you to do, even when others do not. Courage is standing up for what is right. Courage is not giving up, when something is difficult. The greatest thing about courage is that God is ready to help you face any situation, anytime and anywhere.

**Dear God,
Thank You for
helping me to be
courageous.**

So...

So the people said to Joshua, "We will worship the LORD our God and obey him." Joshua 24:24

How do you know when someone really loves you? Do they tell you? Are they nice to you? Do they do good things for you?

You can show God how much you love Him the same way you show a person. Tell God that you love Him. Obey Him by doing what the Bible says. Serve God by loving others the way He loves you. Loving God is so much more than reading about Him or going to church.

**Dear God,
Help me obey
Your Word and
love others.**

304

Not Afraid

Do not fear, for I am with you; do not be afraid, for I am your God. I will strengthen you; I will help you. Isaiah 41:10

What kinds of things scare you the most? Maybe you are afraid of bugs, spiders, the dark, or needles at the doctor's office. Do you know why God wants you to trust Him when you are afraid? It's because nothing scares Him. No matter how scary it may seem to you, nothing frightens God.

Dear God,
Thank You for
helping me to
face the things
that scare me.

305

Our Special Place

When you pray, go into your private room, shut your door, and pray to your Father who is in secret. And your Father who sees in secret will reward you. Matthew 6:6

My son has a special place he goes to read the Bible and pray. That place is behind a bookshelf in the corner of his room. No one can see him there. Kaden discovered that being alone helps him think about God.

Do you have a special place where you go to talk with God? When you take the time to talk with God, you can be sure He is listening. He will teach you so you can help others know Him too. He loves being with you!

Dear God,
Thank You for
hearing me
when I pray.

Good to Be Forgiven

Everyone who calls on the name of the
Lord will be saved. *Romans 10:13*

Trey was both excited and nervous. Today he was
going to tell everyone at church that he had trusted
Jesus to forgive him of his sins. He felt so close
to God since praying with his parents last week to
become a Christian. He finally understood that asking others to forgive him for doing wrong was not
enough. He realized that he never asked God to forgive him. Trey felt relieved to tell God he was sorry
for his sins. How wonderful it felt to be completely
forgiven!

**Dear God,
I want to tell others
that You have saved
me from my sins!**

Words to Live By

The instruction of the LORD is perfect,
renewing one's life. *Psalm 19:7*

King David loved to write songs about God. You can read some of his songs in the book of Psalms. God's words and teachings were important to David. He knew God's instructions could help him live wisely and joyfully.

God's instructions are always true. They are helpful for everyone. If you want to be wise, read the Bible. If you want encouragement, read the Bible. Whatever you need, God's Word can help you. As you learn about God, you can live for Him and tell others about Him.

**Dear God,
Teach me from the
Bible how I should
live for You.**

308

Best Friend Forever

God is faithful; you were called by him into fellowship with his Son, Jesus Christ our Lord. 1 Corinthians 1:9

God loves you. He sent Jesus so you could be forgiven of your sins. God promised Jesus would always be your friend. He will always be with you. He will never disappoint you.

As a Christian, Jesus becomes your best friend, Savior, and Lord.

Dear God,
Thank You that
Jesus is my friend.

309

Serve Others

This is how we have come to know love: He laid down his life for us. We should also lay down our lives for our brothers and sisters. 1 John 3:16

Soren and Carla were in the backyard looking up at the clouds.

"I do not know what to do now," said Carla.

"Girls, come help me pick up the trash that blew into Mr. Harrison's yard last night," said Dad.

"Why?" asked Soren and Carla.

"God wants us to help others. Mr. Harrison needs our help," Dad said.

"Oh, okay! Let's go," they said.

**Dear God,
Please help me
serve others.**

310

Have Mercy!

Keep yourselves in the love of God, waiting expectantly for the mercy of our Lord Jesus Christ for eternal life. Jude 1:21

Some baseball leagues have a *mercy rule*. If one team scores more than 10 runs in one inning, the next team gets to bat, even though they do not have 3 outs. One team is giving *mercy*, or care, to the other team.

In the Bible, *mercy* means "deep caring, forgiveness, and love." Mercy is giving or getting care whether it is deserved or not. Jesus showed mercy to others by being kind to others. So what should we do?

**Dear God,
Help me show
mercy by being
kind to others.**

311

Sing It Again

Day and night they never stop, saying, Holy, holy, holy, Lord God, the Almighty, who was, who is, and who is to come. *Revelation 4:8*

I loved spending the night at my grandparents' house. On Sundays, we would go to their country church where my granddaddy sang in the choir. The songs would get stuck in my head. I would hum the tunes while playing with the farm animals. Often, I would sing aloud. Sundays were such fun!

What fun it would be if we could sing to God all day! The angels do! How joyful they must be! You can be joyful, too, when you keep songs in your heart.

**Dear God,
I will sing so others
can hear how
much I love You.**

Jesus Prays for You

He [Jesus] also is at the right hand of God
and intercedes for us. *Romans 8:34*

Everyone needs help sometimes. Do you? Jesus said He would be your helper at all times. He is powerful and able to help you.

Not only can Jesus help you, but He wants to help you. Jesus listens carefully. Then He prays for you. Jesus is listening and wants to help.

Dear God,
Thank You for
sending Jesus to
be my helper.

God's World

In the beginning God created the heavens and the earth. Genesis 1:1

Sitting on the beach, Mom listened as Kali talked. Then Mom said, "I am so glad you love the beach. Look, what do you see?"

"Clouds. Waves. A funny-looking seagull. Oh, a crab and a shell," said Kali.

"All those things remind us that God is the Creator of the world," Mom explained. "It's like He wrote His name on everything for everyone to see!"

**Dear God,
Thank You for
being our Creator.**

Wisdom

Everyone who hears these words of mine and acts on them will be like a wise man. Matthew 7:24

Being wise means that you obey God and His Word. Following God helps you develop strong friendships, make wise choices, and trust in Him. That's the kind of wisdom you can't find anywhere else!

Dear God,
Help me develop
strong friendships,
make wise choices,
and trust You.

Why Baptize?

Get up and be baptized, and wash away your sins, calling on his [Jesus'] name. Acts 22:16

Emily asked her dad what it means to be baptized. Her dad explained, "Being baptized is showing others that you have already become a Christian. Here's what happens: Jesus died and was buried. So, when you go under the water, that represents being buried with Jesus. Then Jesus rose from the dead to live forever. So when you come up from the water, that represents that you have a new life with God forever."

**Dear God,
Let my baptism
always remind
me of You.**

The Head Over All

And he [God] . . . appointed him [Jesus] as head over everything for the church. *Ephesians 1:22*

"Go right to sleep. We have to get up early to help Pastor Rick's family pack," Mom reminded Anna Grace.

"What's going to happen to our church when Pastor Rick leaves to be a missionary in Asia?" asked Anna Grace.

"The church members work together," said Mom. "Each person has a special part to do. We will continue to serve with our new pastor. But Jesus will always be the head of the church."

Dear God,
Help me serve
You above all.

Worship God

For it is written: Worship the Lord your God, and serve only him. *Matthew 4:10*

Miguel sat next to his friend in church. Miguel's friend made him laugh. Soon Miguel's dad made Miguel move to sit by him.

"Why did you make me move?" Miguel asked later.

"You were not worshiping God," said Dad. "God wants you to focus on Him when you are in church!"

**Dear God,
Help me
worship You!**

318

Listening to God

Come closer and listen to the words of the LORD your God. *Joshua 3:9*

"Listen to my instructions," your teacher says.

"Listen to what I tell you," your dad says.

"I want to tell you what happened today," your sister says.

Lots of people want your attention. But it is most important to listen to God. How can you listen to Him? Read His words in the Bible. When you pray, spend part of your time listening. God wants you to listen!

**Dear God,
Help me listen to You.**

Be Amazed!

When Jesus had finished saying these things, the crowds were astonished at his teaching. *Matthew 7:28*

Jesus was a teacher. When He taught, everyone was amazed. Jesus taught how we should live for God. He taught about being a peacemaker, doing good to others, giving to those in need, and much more. If you read and obey Jesus' words, they will change your life!

**Dear God,
Help me learn
about You.**

Learn from the Best

He was teaching them like one who had authority. *Matthew 7:29*

Have you ever watched a hot-air balloon float across the sky? If you wanted to fly a balloon, how would you learn how to do it? Imagine having a friend who made them and flew them and offered to teach you. Would you feel better if he promised to go with you when you flew?

Balloons are fun, but learning about God is most important. Jesus is the Son of God. Jesus is the best Teacher. He created everything, knows everything, and has power over everything. When Jesus teaches, He has all authority. He wants to be with you and teach you how to live.

**Dear God,
I want to live
for You.**

Turning Cartwheels

Yet I will celebrate in the LORD; I will rejoice in the God of my salvation! *Habakkuk 3:18*

We are all disappointed sometimes. Some disappointments are small, like when your favorite toy breaks. Some disappointments are big, like when your pet fish dies.

When you know God loves you and is able to do all things, you can trust Him. He will give you strength to face disappointments. You can trust Him to make things right one day.

**Dear God,
Thank You for
giving me strength
and hope.**

Honor God

Honor the LORD with your possessions and with the first produce of your entire harvest. *Proverbs 3:9*

Allen looked at the money in his piggy bank. He had enough to buy the new toy he wanted. Allen knew that giving some of his money to the church was the right thing to do. But if he did, he would have to wait until he got more money to buy his toy. All day Allen thought about the toy. But he decided to give to the church. Allen thought, *Giving shows honor and thanks to God!*

Dear God,
Guide me to honor
You with all I have.

Reverence and Awe

Let us be thankful. By it, we may serve God acceptably, with reverence and awe. *Hebrews 12:28*

Ben sat down with his parents in the worship center. He put his Bible next to him. Around Ben, people were saying hello to each other.

During the worship time, Ben sang the songs. While the pastor prayed, Ben thought his own prayer. He thanked God for his family and for loving him. He asked God to help him be still and listen. Ben was happy to be in church worshiping God.

**Dear God,
Remind me to
worship You with
a good attitude.**

Joyful Things

The LORD had done great things for us; we were joyful. *Psalm 126:3*

McKenna saw bright, fluffy clouds on her way to the park. She was exited to play with her friends. Then McKenna remembered she had forgotten to bring her big bouncy ball. But McKenna's mom had remembered. McKenna was happy!

That night McKenna helped her mom set the table. She hummed as she worked. Suddenly McKenna thought, *God has done wonderful things for me today—today and every day!*

Dear God,
The things You do for
me make me very
happy. Thank You.

God's Word

I delight in your commands, which
I love. *Psalm 119:47*

Kyla was so excited to get a new Bible for her birthday. When her mom gave her the Bible, Kyla held it up so everyone at the party could see it and kissed it! Then she hugged it! Kyla couldn't wait for her mom and dad to read her the stories so she could learn more about God.

Dear God,
I love Your words
in the Bible.
Thank You.

Only One God

Now, LORD our God, please save us from his power
so that all the kingdoms of the earth may know
that you, LORD, are God—you alone. *2 Kings 19:19*

Cliff and his dad walked into the pet store. Cliff saw
a dish of fruit. It was sitting next to a small statue.

"Dad," Cliff whispered. "What is that?"

Dad answered, "That is an offering to an idol. The
idol has no real power. The Bible says there is only
one God, the Lord."

"Let's pray for the store owners," said Cliff.

**Dear God,
I praise You for
being the only
real God.**

327

Always There

God is our refuge and strength, a helper who is always found in times of trouble. Psalm 46:1

Kyle was excited to go to Sunday school. He really like his teacher. Mr. Steve always smiled and helped him with the art projects. When Kyle got to church, he found out his teacher was sick and wasn't there that morning. Kyle didn't know the new teacher.

God is always ready to listen and help. He is never sick, gone, or too busy to care. God is the "helper who is always found."

**Dear God,
Thank You for
always being
ready to help me.**

328

Jesus Thanked God

Then Jesus took the loaves, and after giving thanks he distributed them to those who were seated—so also with the fish, as much as they wanted. John 6:11

In November, we think about the first Thanksgiving. The Pilgrims had a difficult first year. They were often hungry. But the Pilgrims thanked God for all He had given them.

Today's verse tells us that Jesus took loaves of bread and thanked God. After His prayer, a miracle happened. The loaves were enough to feed more than 5,000 people!

**Dear God,
Thank You for all
Your gifts to me.**

329

Thanks

Give thanks in everything; for this is God's will for you in Christ Jesus. *1 Thessalonians 5:18*

"I made a thank-you card for Grandma," said Emma. "I love the present she gave me!"

"I forgot to thank her," Logan said. "I will write a thank-you note too."

Sometimes you forget to thank people when they do something for you. Sometimes you forget to thank God too. God cares for you. He gives you good things every day. Thank Him.

**Dear God,
Thank You for
all You do.**

A Hidden Book

Go and inquire of the LORD . . . about the
words in this book. *2 Kings 22:13*

When Josiah became king, he led the people to fix
the temple for worship. The workers in the temple
found a book. The king's secretary brought the
book to Josiah and read it to him. When King Josiah
heard the book of the law, he knew that he and his
people had not obeyed God. He sent his servant to
ask what God would do.

God said, "You listened to My Word. You humbled yourself. I will not punish the people while you
live."

King Josiah then led the people to follow God's
instructions from His Word.

**Dear God,
Thank You for
teaching me
through Your Word.**

Change

Look, I am with you and will watch over you wherever you go. . . . For I will not leave you until I have done what I have promised you. *Genesis 28:15*

Some changes in life can be difficult, like moving to a new house or moving from one town to another. When things get tough or when things change, sticking together as a family is important.

Remember that God is always there to help you and your family.

**Dear God,
Thank You for being
with me when
things change.**

332

Never Alone

No one will be able to stand against you as long as you live. I will be with you, just as I was with Moses. I will not leave you or abandon you. *Joshua 1:5*

Dad walked by Keisha's room and saw her sitting alone, her shoulders shaking. "What is wrong?" Dad asked.

"I am sad that we are moving," Keisha said quietly. "I will not have any friends in my neighborhood. I will not know anyone at church."

Dad hugged Keisha. "God has promised never to leave you. He will help you meet new people and make new friends. Let's pray and ask God to help you make new friends quickly. Always remember that God is with you too," whispered Dad.

Dear God,
Thank You for
never leaving me.

333

Sit, Move, Learn

Teach them to your children, talking about them when you sit in your house and when you walk along the road, when you lie down and when you get up. Deuteronomy 11:19

When you are listening to your parents read you a story, do you like to . . .

- Sit still in a chair?
- Move around using your whole body?
- Snuggle on your bed?

God wants you to know about Him. People in your family and church can help you learn.

**Dear God,
Thank You for
helping me learn.**

Hard to Do

Just as the Lord has forgiven you, so you are also to forgive. Colossians 3:13

Taylor overheard some girls making fun of her. Taylor was sad and her feelings were hurt. Taylor thought those girls were her friends. Taylor thought, *I know I need to forgive them. God has forgiven all the wrong things I have done. I think I will ask God to help me forgive them.* Taylor knows that God will show her what to do.

**Dear God,
Teach me how
to forgive.**

Everyone Everywhere

Every tongue will confess that Jesus Christ is Lord. *Philippians 2:11*

Mika was taking a walk with her mom. When they passed Mrs. Belmonte's house, they heard her singing about Jesus in Spanish. Mika knew the song, so she began singing too in English. Mika's mom knew how to speak French so she started singing along in that language. People from all over the world worship Jesus and praise Him.

**Dear God,
I pray people
everywhere will
trust Jesus as
their Savior.**

God's Plan

One will come from you to be ruler
over Israel for me. *Micah 5:2*

Micah was a prophet who lived about 700 years
before Jesus was born. A prophet is a person God
called to bring His messages to the people. One of
the messages Micah brought was that Jesus would
be born in the city of Bethlehem. Jesus would come
to earth to teach about God's love and to die for the
sins of all people. Jesus came to earth just as the
prophets said.

**Dear God,
Thank You for
planning to send Jesus
long before I ever
knew about You.**

337

God Is with Us

The Lord himself will give you a sign:
See, the virgin will . . . have a son, and
name him Immanuel. *Isaiah 7:14*

The message of Jesus' coming was so important that God had more than one prophet tell about Jesus' birth. God sent another prophet named Isaiah. Isaiah lived and taught about 700 years before Jesus was born. Isaiah told that one of Jesus' names would be Immanuel. *Immanuel* means "God is with us."

Dear God,
Thank You for
sending Jesus and
giving Him the
name Immanuel.

God's Promise

A child will be born for us. *Isaiah 9:6*

Today's verse reminds us that God will do what He promised. He told His people, the Israelites, that He would send a Savior. God had Isaiah tell the people the Savior would be born as a baby. Isaiah knew that the people were looking forward to Jesus' coming. Isaiah wanted them to know that they could count on God. God always keeps His promises.

Dear God,
Thank You for
always keeping
Your promises.

339

God's Timing

When the time came to completion,
God sent his Son, born of a woman,
born under the law. Galatians 4:4

Do you ever feel like God should do something right now? We have probably all had that feeling. The Israelites wanted the Messiah right then! They had been waiting for years.

God sent Jesus right on time. He knew we needed a way to be forgiven for our sins. We can be glad that God's timing is perfect.

Dear God,
Thank You for
always being
right on time.

340

Immanuel

The virgin will . . . give birth to a son, and they will name him Immanuel, which is translated "God is with us." Matthew 1:23

God wants you to learn about Him. He wants you to love Him because of who He is and what He does. God often teaches a truth over and over in the Bible. He wants to make sure you understand what He is teaching. More than once God reminds us that one of Jesus' names is *Immanuel,* which means "God is with us!"

When you learn about Jesus, you see what God is like.

**Dear God,
Thank You for sending
Jesus and showing
me, through Him,
what You are like.**

Rejoice

The angel came to her [Mary] and said, "Greetings, favored woman! The Lord is with you." *Luke 1:28*

God chose Mary to be Jesus' mother. God sent an angel to tell her about His plan for her. Do you think Mary was afraid when she saw and heard the angel? Absolutely!

God knows when you are afraid. But, just like Mary, you can be sure that He will help you not be afraid. You have been chosen by God to learn about Jesus and to follow Him.

**Dear God,
Thank You for helping me
not be afraid of things
I do not understand.**

God's Son

He will be great and will be called the
Son of the Most High. Luke 1:32

Jesus is more than just a good man. Today's verse reminds us that He is the Son of the Most High. In other words, Jesus is God's Son. He is a good teacher! He is a good shepherd! He is Immanuel! But most importantly, He is God's Son.

What does it mean to say that someone is great? Whatever you say, Jesus is all of those things and more.

Dear God,
Thank You for
sending Your
Son, Jesus, to be
my Savior.

God's Spirit Works

The Holy Spirit will come upon you, and . . . the holy one to be born will be called the Son of God. Luke 1:35

Sometimes God teaches you through the Bible. Sometimes He teaches you through teachers, pastors, and your parents. In today's verse, God works through His Spirit to bring Jesus to earth.

The Holy Spirit helped Mary to have a baby. The baby is God's Son. The baby grew to be a boy, then a man, and then did things that only God's Son could do.

**Dear God,
Thank You for
sending the Holy
Spirit to work
in my life.**

Only God

Nothing will be impossible with God. Luke 1:37

God can do anything He wants to do. He created the world and everything in it. He made people. He knew that when Adam and Eve sinned, they would need a Savior.

God did what no one else could do. He sent His Son Jesus to earth to teach us about God and His love. Jesus became our Savior.

**Dear God,
Thank You that You
can do anything You
want to do. Thank
You for being God.**

Pure Words

Every word of God is pure. Proverbs 30:5

If you find something floating in your drinking water, don't you dump it out and pour pure, clean water into your cup?

The same should be true for what you believe. Shouldn't you be certain that what you are being taught is pure? The only way to keep your belief about God pure is to keep reading and believing the Bible.

**Dear God,
Help me follow
only Your Word.**

God's Best Gift

Thanks be to God for his indescribable gift! 2 Corinthians 9:15

Dean gave his Christmas list to his mom.

She quickly read the list. "These are all things you want. But what about making a list of things you can give to others? When God sent Jesus, He gave us the best gift ever. What can you give to show thanks to God?" she asked.

Dean later brought another list:

- I can give a special offering to missions.
- I can help collect toys for the homeless shelter.
- I can _____ (write your own gift idea).

**Dear God,
Thank You for
the awesome
gift of Jesus.**

God Wants Our Best

"I am the Lord's servant," said Mary. "May it be done to me according to your word." Then the angel left her. *Luke 1:38*

This verse uses the word, *servant*. What do you think of when you think of someone being a servant? In our world, servants are often not given much respect.

Today's verse teaches that Mary thought of herself as a *servant*, "one who serves God and knows that God knows best for her." Mary knew from the angel's message that God respected her and wanted what was best for her.

**Dear God,
I can show You
that I love You by
doing what You
want me to do.**

Mary Obeyed God

He has looked with favor on . . . his servant. Surely, from now on all generations will call me blessed. *Luke 1:48*

God chose Mary to be the mother of His Son. Mary wanted to obey God and follow His plan. This verse teaches us that Mary obeyed God. You can follow Mary's example and obey and follow God.

We are blessed because Mary chose to obey God. And you will bless others when you choose to obey God.

Dear God,
Thank You for
choosing Mary.
Thank You for
choosing me.

349

Jesus' Birthday

While they were there, the time came for her to give birth. Luke 2:6

When is your birthday? It is at the time God chose. You were born exactly when God wanted you to be born. How do you feel when your family and friends celebrate your birthday?

Jesus, too, was born exactly when God wanted Him to be born. We do not know that it was actually on December 25. But the important thing is that we take time to honor His birth.

**Dear God,
Thank You for Jesus'
birthday. Thank You
for my birthday.**

350

The Stable

She gave birth to her firstborn Son, and she wrapped him tightly in cloth and laid him in a manger, because there was no guest room available for them. *Luke 2:7*

The night Jesus was born, His parents did not stay in a fancy hotel. Mary and Joseph spent the night where animals were kept.

There were no nice beds for them. They did not have a baby bed for Jesus. They only had a trough where straw was placed for the animals to eat. Jesus slept there.

**Dear God,
Thank You for taking care of Mary and Joseph on the night Baby Jesus was born.**

The Shepherds

An angel of the Lord stood before them, and the glory of the Lord shone around them, and they were terrified. *Luke 2:9*

When you have good news, who is the first person you tell? God chose to tell the shepherds first about the birth of the Savior.

God loves everyone. He does not choose to love a person because of the job that person holds. Even though the shepherds were afraid, they were happy the angels told them the good news.

**Dear God,
Thank You for
loving us all
the same.**

352

Good News

The angel said to them, "Don't be afraid, for look, I proclaim to you good news of great joy that will be for all the people." Luke 2:10

Today's verse is one of the places we find the phrase *good news*. This good news is about Jesus. God sent Jesus to teach us about God, die on the cross for our sins, and become the Savior of the world.

Are you thinking about becoming a follower of Jesus? If so, pray and talk with God about it.

**Dear God,
Help me understand
more about Jesus
and the good news
He brings us.**

Messiah

Today in the city of David a Savior was born for you, who is the Messiah, the Lord. Luke 2:11

The word *Messiah* in the Bible talks about a Savior. Jesus came to be the Messiah for everyone.

The Jewish people waited and looked for the Messiah. But God's plan was for Jesus to be the Savior for everyone. As you learn about Jesus and all that He has done for you, you can choose to follow Him.

Dear God,
Help me learn more
about Jesus, the
Messiah, Your Son.

Worship

Let all God's angels worship him. Hebrews 1:6

God commands the angels to worship Jesus. Angels are created by God to worship Him and His Son.

Should we worship God and Jesus like the angels do? Yes! God wants you to worship Him. Try the following ways:

- Tell God how much you love Him and Jesus.
- Tell God how thankful you are for all He does for you.

Dear God,
I love You. Thank You
for sending Jesus. Jesus,
thank You for dying on
the cross for my sin.

The First to Hear

The shepherds said to one another, "Let's go straight to Bethlehem and see what has happened, which the Lord has made known to us." Luke 2:15

People often hurry to the hospital to see a newborn family member. They have probably waited for the birth and are so excited that the baby is here.

The shepherds were happy to hear the good news of Jesus' birth. They had been waiting for the Messiah to be born. The Messiah is the Savior of the world. Can you imagine being the first to find out about Jesus' birth? How exciting!

**Dear God,
Thank You that You
want everyone
to know about
Jesus' birth.**

Go and Tell

*After seeing them, they reported the message
they were told about this child. Luke 2:17*

The shepherds hurried to Bethlehem to find Baby
Jesus just like the angel said. They found Jesus and
they worshiped Him. Then they hurried out to tell
others about the Messiah's birth.

The shepherds did not keep the good news
about Jesus a secret. Should we? No, we should
be happy and proud to tell others what we have
learned about Jesus.

**Dear God,
Help me to be
willing to tell
others the good
news about Jesus.**

The Christmas Star

And there it was—the star they had seen at its rising. It led them until it came and stopped above the place where the child was. Matthew 2:9

God used the star to lead a group of wise men from east of Jerusalem to come and see the newborn King Jesus. They probably arrived in Bethlehem up to two years after Jesus was born. By the time they arrived, Jesus was probably a toddler. God uses lots of things and people to help you learn about Jesus.

**Dear God,
Thank You for sending
the Christmas star to
guide men to Jesus.**

Joy

When they saw the star, they were overwhelmed with joy. *Matthew 2:10*

We use a lot of words to tell how we feel about finding Jesus: *excited*, *glad*, *happy*, *thankful*, *amazed*. But one of the best words to use when talking about the birth of Jesus and what it means is the word *joy*.

Do you know the song "Joy to the World"? What about stopping right now to sing a Christmas song that brings you joy?

**Dear God,
fill me with joy
when I think
about Jesus.**

359

One Verse

For God loved the world in this way: He gave his one and only Son, so that everyone who believes in him will not perish but have eternal life. *John 3:16*

The whole Christmas story is told in this one verse. God loves you. He knows you have sinned. He sent Jesus to die on the cross for your sins. You can believe in Jesus and ask Him to forgive your sins. You can become a lifelong follower of Jesus.

Have you memorized this verse yet? Why not give yourself a Christmas gift and memorize John 3:16?

Dear God,
Help me learn
this verse and
understand
what it means.

360

Something to Think About

Mary was treasuring up all these things in her heart and meditating on them. Luke 2:19

Christmas is a time to celebrate Jesus' birth. We celebrate in times of eating, worshiping, giving gifts, and going to parties.

Mary did more than celebrate the birth of God's Son. She meditated on, or thought about, what it meant that God's Son had been born. Make a list of things to think about during the Christmas season. Your list might include things that remind you how much God loves you.

**Dear God,
Help me remember
all of the wonderful
things about Jesus.**

Proud Parents

His father and mother were amazed at what was being said about him. Luke 2:33

Joseph and Mary were very proud parents. They felt happy that God sent His Son. They were glad to hear people call Jesus the Messiah.

Your parents, grandparents, and family are probably proud of you too! You were born as a baby like Jesus was born as a baby. You will grow like Jesus grew and get smarter, taller, and friendlier. But the most important thing you will do is learn about Jesus.

**Dear God,
Help me learn
more and more
about Jesus.**

362

God's Plan

What we have seen and heard we also declare to you. 1 John 1:3

God's plan is that people who know Jesus will tell others about Him.

Just think. If the first Christians had not told others about Jesus, no one today would know about His life!

Do you know the story of Jesus' birth? Do you know a miracle Jesus did? Those are things you can tell people around you.

You are part of God's plan for telling others about Him.

**Dear God,
Thank You for
Your plan to tell
others about You.**

Gift of God

The gift of God is eternal life in Christ Jesus our Lord. *Romans 6:23*

The Bible teaches you about eternal life, and how to become a part of God's forever family. How do you do that?

- You learn about Jesus.
- You ask Him to forgive you for your sins.
- You accept His forgiveness as a gift.
- You ask Jesus to become Lord, or boss, of your life and to help you make good choices about obeying God.

What a gift!

**Dear God,
Help me understand
Your perfect
gift of Jesus.**

364

God's Patience

The Lord . . . is patient with you, not wanting any to perish. *2 Peter 3:9*

God wants every person to be part of His forever family. He teaches about His love by helping us understand who Jesus is and what He has done for us. God wants everyone to believe that Jesus is His Son and that Jesus did what is needed to help us receive forgiveness for our sins.

Talk to a parent or teacher if you have questions about becoming a Christian.

**Dear God,
Help me understand
what it means to
become a Christian.**

Worthy of Worship

The whole earth will worship you and sing praise to you. They will sing praise to your name. *Psalm 66:4*

All month we have been talking about God's Son, Jesus. Christmas is a special time to remember that Jesus was born as a baby. He came to teach us how to live our lives. He also came to die for our sins. How exciting it is to begin a new year praising God for who He is and what He did in sending Jesus.

**Dear God,
Help me spend time
praising You and
thanking You for Jesus.**